The Wiersbe BIBLE STUDY SERIES

ECCLESIASTES

The
Wiersbe
BIBLE STUDY SERIES

Looking for
the Answer
to the
Meaning of Life

David C Cook
transforming lives together

THE WIERSBE BIBLE STUDY SERIES: ECCLESIASTES
Published by David C Cook
4050 Lee Vance View
Colorado Springs, CO 80918 U.S.A.

David C Cook Distribution Canada
55 Woodslee Avenue, Paris, Ontario, Canada N3L 3E5

David C Cook U.K., Kingsway Communications
Eastbourne, East Sussex BN23 6NT, England

ISBN 978-0-7814-0842-4
eISBN 978-1-4347-0519-8

The Team: Steve Parolini, Karen Lee-Thorp, Amy Konyndyk,
Nick Lee, Jack Campbell, Karen Athen
Series Cover Design: John Hamilton Design
Cover Photo: Shutterstock

Printed in the United States of America
First Edition 2012

1 2 3 4 5 6 7 8 9 10

082712

Contents

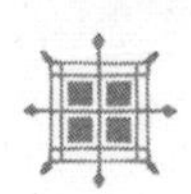

Introduction to Ecclesiastes

Satisfaction

"Life is filled with difficulties and perplexities," King Solomon concluded, "and there's much that nobody can understand, let alone control. From the human point of view, it's all vanity and folly. But life is God's gift to us, and He wants us to enjoy it and use it for His glory."

Fullness

Our Jewish friends read Ecclesiastes at the annual Feast of Tabernacles, a joyful autumn festival of harvest. It fits! For Solomon wrote, "A man can do nothing better than to eat and drink and find satisfaction in his work. This too, I see, is from the hand of God" (Eccl. 2:24). Even the apostle Paul (who could hardly be labeled a hedonist) said that God "richly provides us with everything for our enjoyment" (1 Tim. 6:17).

Life without Jesus Christ is indeed "meaningless, a chasing after the wind" (Eccl. 1:14). But when you know Him personally, and live for Him faithfully, you experience fullness of joy and pleasures forever more (Ps. 16:11).

Instead of complaining about what you don't have, start giving thanks for what you do have—and be satisfied!

—*Warren W. Wiersbe*

How to Use This Study

This study is designed for both individual and small-group use. We've divided it into eight lessons—each references one or more chapters in Warren W. Wiersbe's commentary *Be Satisfied* (second edition, David C Cook, 2010). While reading *Be Satisfied* is not a prerequisite for going through this study, the additional insights and background Wiersbe offers can greatly enhance your study experience.

The **Getting Started** questions at the beginning of each lesson offer you an opportunity to record your first thoughts and reactions to the study text. This is an important step in the study process as those "first impressions" often include clues about what it is your heart is longing to discover.

The bulk of the study is found in the **Going Deeper** questions. These dive into the Bible text and, along with helpful excerpts from Wiersbe's commentary, help you examine not only the original context and meaning of the verses but also modern application.

Looking Inward narrows the focus down to your personal story. These intimate questions can be a bit uncomfortable at times, but don't shy away from honesty here. This is where you are asked to stand before the mirror of God's Word and look closely at what you see. It's the place to take a good look at yourself in light of the lesson and search for ways in which you can grow in faith.

Going Forward is the place where you can commit to paper those things you want or need to do in order to better live out the discoveries you made in the Looking Inward section. Don't skip or skim through this. Take the time to really consider what practical steps you might take to move closer to Christ. Then share your thoughts with a trusted friend who can act as an encourager and accountability partner.

Finally, there is a brief **Seeking Help** section to close the lesson. This is a reminder for you to invite God into your spiritual-growth process. If you choose to write out a prayer in this section, come back to it as you work through the lesson and continue to seek the Holy Spirit's guidance as you discover God's will for your life.

Tips for Small Groups

A small group is a dynamic thing. One week it might seem like a group of close-knit friends. The next it might seem more like a group of uncomfortable strangers. A small-group leader's role is to read these subtle changes and adjust the tone of the discussion accordingly.

Small groups need to be safe places for people to talk openly. It is through shared wrestling with difficult life issues that some of the greatest personal growth is discovered. But in order for the group to feel safe, participants need to know it's okay *not* to share sometimes. Always invite honest disclosure, but never force someone to speak if he or she isn't comfortable doing so. (A savvy leader will follow up later with a group member who isn't comfortable sharing in a group setting to see if a one-on-one discussion is more appropriate.)

Have volunteers take turns reading excerpts from Scripture or from the commentary. The more each person is involved even in the mundane tasks, the more they'll feel comfortable opening up in more meaningful ways.

The leader should watch the clock and keep the discussion moving. Sometimes there may be more Going Deeper questions than your group can cover in your available time. If you've had a fruitful discussion, it's okay to move on without finishing everything. And if you think the group is getting bogged down on a question or has taken off on a tangent, you can simply say, "Let's go on to question 5." Be sure to save at least ten to fifteen minutes for the Going Forward questions.

Finally, soak your group meetings in prayer—before you begin, during as needed, and always at the end of your time together.

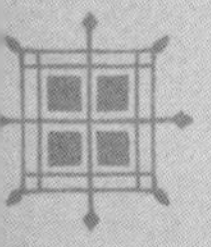

Worth Living
(ECCLESIASTES 1)

Before you begin …

- *Pray for the Holy Spirit to reveal truth and wisdom as you go through this lesson.*
- *Read Ecclesiastes 1. This lesson references chapters 1 and 2 in* Be Satisfied. *It will be helpful for you to have your Bible and a copy of the commentary available as you work through this lesson.*

Getting Started

From the Commentary

"Vanity of vanities," lamented Solomon, "all is vanity!" Solomon liked that word *vanity*; he used it thirty-eight times in Ecclesiastes as he wrote about life "under the sun." The word means "emptiness, futility, vapor, that which vanishes quickly and leaves nothing behind."

From the human point of view ("under the sun"), life does appear futile; and it is easy for us to get pessimistic.

The Jewish writer Sholom Aleichem once described life as "a blister on top of a tumor, and a boil on top of that." You can almost *feel* that definition!

The American poet Carl Sandburg compared life to "an onion—you peel it off one layer at a time, and sometimes you weep." And British playwright George Bernard Shaw said that life was "a series of inspired follies."

What a relief to turn from these pessimistic views and hear Jesus Christ say, "I am come that they might have life, and that they might have it more abundantly" (John 10:10). Or to read Paul's majestic declaration, "Therefore, my beloved brethren, be steadfast, immovable, always abounding in the work of the Lord, knowing that your labor is not in vain in the Lord" (1 Cor. 15:58 NKJV).

—*Be Satisfied*, pages 15–16

1. Why do you think Solomon used the word *vanity* (or *meaningless* NIV) so often? (Underline all the uses as you go through Ecclesiastes.) How did he use repetition to drive home his point? How is this main point applicable to today's world?

More to Consider: Nowhere in Ecclesiastes did the author give his name, but the descriptions he gave of himself and his experiences indicate that the writer was King Solomon. Read Ecclesiastes 1:1, 12–13; 2:1–11; and 1 Kings 4:20–34; 10:1–20. How do these verses support the idea of Solomon's authorship? Is his authorship critical to the content? Why or why not? How would the value of Ecclesiastes change (if at all) had another author written it?

2. Choose one verse or phrase from Ecclesiastes 1 that stands out to you. This could be something you're intrigued by, something that makes you uncomfortable, something that puzzles you, something that resonates with you, or just something you want to examine further. Write that here.

Going Deeper

From the Commentary

Ecclesiastes appears to be the kind of book a person would write near the close of life, reflecting on life's experiences and the lessons learned. Solomon probably wrote Proverbs (Prov. 1:1; 1 Kings 4:32) and the Song of Solomon (1:1) during the years he faithfully walked with God, and near the end of his life, he wrote Ecclesiastes. There is no record

> that King Solomon repented and turned to the Lord, but his message in Ecclesiastes suggests that he did.
>
> He wrote Proverbs from the viewpoint of a wise teacher (1:1–6), and Song of Solomon from the viewpoint of a royal lover (3:7–11), but when he wrote Ecclesiastes, he called himself "the Preacher" (1:1, 2, 12; 7:27; 12:8–10). The Hebrew word is *koheleth* (ko-HAY-leth) and is the title given to an official speaker who calls an assembly (see 1 Kings 8:1). The Greek word for "assembly" is *ekklesia*, and this gives us the English title of the book, Ecclesiastes.
>
> —*Be Satisfied*, pages 17–18

3. What are some of the clues to suggest Solomon wrote this near the end of his life? Why did he refer to himself as "the Preacher" (or "the Teacher" NIV) in Ecclesiastes? What does this say about the audience for his words?

From the Commentary

> Solomon has put the key to Ecclesiastes right at the front door: "Vanity of vanities, saith the Preacher, vanity of vanities; all is vanity. What profit hath a man of

all his labour which he taketh under the sun?" (1:2–3). Just in case we missed it, he put the same key at the back door (12:8). In these verses, Solomon introduces some of the key words and phrases that are used repeatedly in Ecclesiastes, so we had better get acquainted with them.

Vanity of vanities. We have already noted that Solomon used the word *vanity* thirty-eight times in this book. It is the Hebrew word *hevel*, meaning "emptiness, futility, vapor." The name "Abel" probably comes from this word (Gen. 4:2). Whatever disappears quickly, leaves nothing behind, and does not satisfy is *hevel*, vanity. One of my language professors at seminary defined *hevel* as "whatever is left after you break a soap bubble."

Whether he considers his wealth, his works, his wisdom, or his world, Solomon comes to the same sad conclusion: all is "vanity and vexation of spirit" (2:11). However, this is not his final conclusion, nor is it the only message that he has for his readers. We will discover more about that later.

Under the sun. You will find this important phrase twenty-nine times in Ecclesiastes, and with it the phrase "under heaven" (1:13; 2:3; 3:1). It defines the outlook of the writer as he looks at life from a human perspective and not necessarily from heaven's point of view. He applies his own wisdom and experience to the complex human situation and tries to make some sense out of life. Solomon wrote under the inspiration of the Holy Spirit (12:10–11; 2 Tim. 3:16), so what he wrote was what God wanted His

> people to have. But as we study, we must keep Solomon's viewpoint in mind: he is examining life "under the sun."
>
> —*Be Satisfied*, pages 18–19

4. Why is it important to be aware of Solomon's "human perspective" when reading Ecclesiastes? How is this similar to and different from reading Proverbs? Song of Solomon?

From the Commentary

> In spite of his painful encounters with the world and its problems, Solomon does not recommend either pessimism or cynicism. Rather, he admonishes us to be realistic about life, accept God's gifts, and enjoy them (2:24; 3:12–15, 22; 5:18–20; 8:15; 9:7–10; 11:9–10). After all, God gives to us "richly all things to enjoy" (1 Tim. 6:17). Words related to joy (enjoy, rejoice, etc.) are used at least seventeen times in Ecclesiastes. Solomon does not say, "Eat, drink, and be merry, for tomorrow you die!" Instead, he advises us to trust God and enjoy what we *do* have rather than complain about what we *don't* have. Life

> is short and life is difficult, so make the most of it while you can.
>
> —*Be Satisfied*, page 20

5. How did Solomon present the message of "joy" in a book so rife with messages that seem so cynical? Why might some readers of Ecclesiastes have a hard time seeing that message? How do we get from cynicism to joy?

From the Commentary

> The message in Ecclesiastes is for today. After all, the society which Solomon investigated a millennium before the birth of Christ was not too different from our world today. Solomon saw injustice to the poor (4:1–3), crooked politics (5:8), incompetent leaders (10:6–7), guilty people allowed to commit more crime (8:11), materialism (5:10), and a desire for "the good old days" (7:10). It sounds up-to-date, doesn't it?
>
> If you have never trusted Jesus Christ as your Savior, then this book urges you to do so without delay. Why? Because no matter how much wealth, education, or social prestige

> you may have, life without God is futile. You are only "chasing after the wind" if you expect to find satisfaction and personal fulfillment in the things of the world. "For what shall it profit a man, if he should gain the whole world, and lose his own soul?" asked Jesus (Mark 8:36).
>
> —*Be Satisfied*, page 22

6. What are some of the practical applications of Ecclesiastes for us today? Why is it of particular relevance in modern America?

From the Commentary

> "Everything an Indian does is in a circle," said Black Elk, the Sioux religious leader. "Even the seasons form a great circle in their changing and always come back again to where they were. The life of a man is a circle from childhood to childhood."
>
> You would think Black Elk had been studying the first chapter of Ecclesiastes, except for one fact: For centuries, wise men and women in different nations and cultures have been pondering the mysteries of the "circles" of

> human life. Whenever you use phrases like "life cycle," or "the wheel of fortune," or "come full circle," you are joining Solomon and Black Elk and a host of others in taking a cyclical view of life and nature.
>
> —*Be Satisfied*, page 27

7. Why was the cyclical view of life a burden to Solomon? How did he answer the question "If life is only part of a circle, is it worth living?" (See Eccl. 1:4–18.) Where is this cyclical view of life used in modern society? What makes it appealing to some?

From the Commentary

> In Ecclesiastes 1:4–7, Solomon approached the problem as a scientist and examined the "wheel of nature" around him: the earth, the sun, the wind, and the water. (This reminds us of the ancient "elements" of earth, air, fire, and water.) He was struck by the fact that generations of people came and went, while the things of nature remained. There was "change" all around, yet nothing really changed. Everything was only part of the "wheel

> of nature" and contributed to the monotony of life. So, Solomon asked, "Is life worth living?"
>
> —*Be Satisfied*, page 28

8. What evidence did Solomon present to prove that nothing really changes? Why is this conclusion important to Solomon's greater message to accept and enjoy God's gifts?

More to Consider: God does break into nature to do great and wonderful things! Read the following verses and note how God did this in each example: Joshua 3—4; 10:6–14; Isaiah 38:1–8; Exodus 14; 1 Kings 17; James 5:17–18; Mark 4:35–41.

From the Commentary

> If nothing changes, then it is reasonable to conclude that nothing in this world is new. This "logical conclusion" might have satisfied people in Solomon's day, but it startles us today. After all, we are surrounded by, and

> dependent on, a multitude of marvels that modern science has provided for us—everything from telephones to pacemakers and miracle drugs. How could anybody who watched Neil Armstrong walk on the moon agree with Solomon that nothing is new under the sun?
>
> —*Be Satisfied*, page 30

9. Review Ecclesiastes 1:8–11. How did Solomon move from scientist to historian in these verses? How did his perspective affect his message? In what ways is it true that nothing changes in human society from generation to generation?

From the Commentary

> In Ecclesiastes 1:12–18, the historian now becomes the philosopher as Solomon tells how he went about searching for the answer to the problem that vexed him. As the king of Israel, he had all the resources necessary for "experimenting" with different solutions to see what it was that made life worth living.
>
> —*Be Satisfied*, page 32

10. What were some of the ways Solomon went searching for the answer to his "Is life all vanity?" questions? How are these similar to the ways people try to find meaning in today's society? Why do these approaches fall short of providing satisfying answers?

Looking Inward

Take a moment to reflect on all that you've explored thus far in this study of Ecclesiastes 1. Review your notes and answers and think about how each of these things matters in your life today.

> *Tips for Small Groups: To get the most out of this section, form pairs or trios and have group members take turns answering these questions. Be honest and as open as you can in this discussion, but most of all, be encouraging and supportive of others. Be sensitive to those who are going through particularly difficult times and don't press for people to speak if they're uncomfortable doing so.*

11. Solomon's reflections seem to come from late in life. What is the value in asking those questions today, no matter how old you are? What are the sorts of questions you hope to be asking as you grow close to the end of your time on earth?

12. What are some things that make you cynical about life? What are some things that give you joy? How can you find joy by reframing the cynicism? What would it look like to live a more joy-focused life?

13. What are some ways you've searched for the answers to Solomon's questions? How has that worked out for you? What have you learned in that process? What does this tell you about the role faith plays in contentment?

Going Forward

14. Think of one or two things that you have learned that you'd like to work on in the coming week. Remember that this is all about quality, not quantity. It's better to work on one specific area of life and do it well than to work on many and do poorly (or to be so overwhelmed that you simply don't try).

Do you want to let go of cynicism about life? Be specific. Go back through Ecclesiastes 1 and put a star next to the phrase or verse that is most encouraging to you. Consider memorizing this verse.

Real-Life Application Ideas: Take a casual survey of friends, coworkers, and even family members, asking, "Where do you find meaning in life?" Don't limit yourself to believers—ask everyone you come in contact with. Share the results with your small group or Sunday school class. Be sure to spend some time talking about how the results might affect your approach to sharing the gospel with others.

Seeking Help

15. Write a prayer below (or simply pray one in silence), inviting God to work on your mind and heart in those areas you've noted in the Going Forward section. Be honest about your desires and fears.

Notes for Small Groups:

- *Look for ways to put into practice the things you wrote in the Going Forward section. Talk with other group members about your ideas and commit to being accountable to one another.*
- *During the coming week, ask the Holy Spirit to continue to reveal truth to you from what you've read and studied.*
- *Before you start the next lesson, read Ecclesiastes 2. For more in-depth lesson preparation, read chapter 3, "Disgusted with Life?," in* Be Satisfied.

Disgust
(ECCLESIASTES 2)

Before you begin …

- *Pray for the Holy Spirit to reveal truth and wisdom as you go through this lesson.*
- *Read Ecclesiastes 2. This lesson references chapter 3 in* Be Satisfied. *It will be helpful for you to have your Bible and a copy of the commentary available as you work through this lesson.*

Getting Started

From the Commentary

"There is but one step from the sublime to the ridiculous." Napoleon is supposed to have made that statement after his humiliating retreat from Moscow in the winter of 1812. The combination of stubborn Russian resistance and a severe Russian winter was too much for the French army, and its expected sublime victory was turned into shameful defeat.

> As part of his quest for "the good life," King Solomon examined everything from the sublime to the ridiculous. In the great laboratory of life, he experimented with one thing after another, always applying the wisdom that God had given him (Eccl. 2:3, 9).
>
> —*Be Satisfied*, page 39

1. What are some of the ridiculous things Solomon examined in his search for meaning? What are some of the sublime solutions he sought out? Why do you think he tried so many different approaches to find the purpose for existence?

2. Choose one verse or phrase from Ecclesiastes 2 that stands out to you. This could be something you're intrigued by, something that makes you uncomfortable, something that puzzles you, something that resonates with you, or just something you want to examine further. Write that here.

Going Deeper

From the Commentary

> Solomon had the means and the authority to do just about anything his heart desired. He decided to test his own heart to see how he would respond to two very common experiences of life: enjoyment (Eccl. 2:1–3) and employment (vv. 4–11).
>
> The Hebrew people rightly believed that God made man to enjoy the blessings of His creation (Ps. 104; and note 1 Tim. 6:17). The harvest season was a joyful time for them as they reaped the blessings of God on their labor. At the conclusion of his book, Solomon admonished his readers to enjoy God's blessings during the years of their youth, before old age arrived and the body began to fall apart (Eccl. 12:1ff.). Eight times in Ecclesiastes, Solomon used the Hebrew word meaning "pleasure," so it is obvious that he did not consider God a celestial spoilsport.
>
> —*Be Satisfied*, pages 39–40

3. How did Solomon respond to his test of enjoyment? Why is it significant that Solomon didn't see God as a "celestial spoilsport"? How does this compare to the way many Christians (and non-Christians) view the Christian faith? In what ways was Solomon on to something in his exploration of enjoyment as a path to meaning?

More to Consider: Solomon specifically mentioned wine and laughter as two sources of pleasure used in his experiment. Read 1 Kings 4:22–23; 10:21; and Ecclesiastes 2:8. How do these verses illustrate this source of pleasure? Why did these pleasures fall short of answering Solomon's questions? How do people today pursue similar sources of pleasure?

From the Commentary

> While there is nothing wrong with innocent fun, the person who builds his or her life only on seeking pleasure is bound to be disappointed in the end.
>
> Why? For one thing, pleasure-seeking usually becomes a selfish endeavor; and selfishness destroys true joy. People who live for pleasure often exploit others to get what they want, and they end up with broken relationships as well as empty hearts. *People are more important than things and thrills.* We are to be channels, not reservoirs; the greatest joy comes when we share God's pleasures with others.
>
> If you live for pleasure alone, enjoyment will decrease unless the intensity of the pleasure increases. Then you reach a point of diminishing returns when there is little or no enjoyment at all, only bondage. For example, the more that people drink, the less enjoyment they get out of it. This means they must have more drinks and stronger drinks in order to have pleasure; the sad result is desire without satisfaction. Instead of alcohol, substitute drugs, gambling, sex, money, fame, or any other pursuit, and

the principle will hold true: When pleasure alone is the center of life, the result will ultimately be disappointment and emptiness.

There is a third reason why pleasure alone can never bring satisfaction: It appeals to only part of the person and ignores the total being. This is the major difference between shallow "entertainment" and true "enjoyment," for when the whole person is involved, there will be both enjoyment and enrichment. Entertainment has its place, but we must keep in mind that it only helps us to escape life temporarily.

—*Be Satisfied*, pages 40–41

4. What makes the pursuit of pleasure a selfish act? In what ways is it incomplete? What is the difference between temporary pleasure and true pleasure?

From Today's World

Today's world is pleasure-crazy. Millions of people will pay almost any amount of money to buy experiences and temporarily escape the burdens of life. From movies to television to video games to sporting events—entertainment isn't just a hallmark of the American life; for many it's the very definition of it. Entertainment industries are billion-dollar income producers, and advertisers bank on this by attempting to appeal to our desire to have fun.

5. Why is the entertainment business so successful in America? Why are we obsessed with having fun? What does this say about our culture? What are the benefits of pursuing pleasure? What are the dangers? How are both evidenced in our society today?

From the Commentary

> In Ecclesiastes 2:4–11, Solomon got involved in all kinds of projects, hoping to discover something that would make life worth living. He started with *great works* (vv. 4–6), including houses (1 Kings 7), cities (2 Chron. 8:4–6), gardens, vineyards, orchards and forests (1 Kings 4:33), and the water systems needed to service them. Of course, Solomon also supervised the construction of the temple (1 Kings 5ff.), one of the greatest buildings of the ancient world.

He not only had works, but he also had *workers* (Eccl. 2:7a). He had two kinds of slaves: those he purchased and those born in his household. He might have added that he "drafted" 30,000 Jewish men to work on various projects (1 Kings 5:13–18). His father David had conscripted the strangers in the land (1 Chron. 22:2), but Solomon drafted his own people, and the people resented it (see 1 Kings 12).

Of course, Solomon accumulated *wealth* (Eccl. 2:7b–8a), in flocks and herds (1 Kings 8:63) as well as gold and silver (1 Kings 4:21; 10:1ff.). He was the wealthiest and wisest man in the whole world, yet he was unhappy because activity alone does not bring lasting pleasure.

—*Be Satisfied*, pages 41–42

6. How can employment help us find purpose and value in life? In what ways did Solomon seek fulfillment through work? How is the pursuit of wealth different from seeking significance through work? What does Solomon's experience teach us about these pursuits?

From the Commentary

> In Ecclesiastes 2:12, "I turned myself to behold" simply means, "I considered things from another viewpoint." What Solomon did was to look at his wisdom (vv. 12–17) and his wealth (vv. 18–23) *in light of the certainty of death.* What good is it to be wise and wealthy if you are going to die and leave everything behind?
>
> The certainty of death is a topic Solomon frequently mentioned in Ecclesiastes (1:4; 2:14–17; 3:18–20; 5:15–16; 6:6; 8:8; 9:2–3, 12; 12:7–8). He could not easily avoid the subject as he looked at life "under the sun," for death is one of the obvious facts of life. The French essayist Montaigne wrote, "Philosophy is no other thing than for a man to prepare himself to death." Only that person is prepared to live who is prepared to die.
>
> —*Be Satisfied*, pages 42–43

7. Skim some of the verses listed in the previous excerpt from *Be Satisfied* where Solomon talked about the certainty of death. Why so much emphasis on this subject? How might his various (and unsuccessful) pursuits have prompted this repeated theme? Is it useful to think about death? Explain.

From the Commentary

Not only did Solomon hate life, but he hated the wealth that was the result of his toil. Of course, Solomon was born wealthy, and great wealth came to him because he was the king. But he was looking at life "under the sun" and speaking for the "common people" who were listening to his discussion. He gave three reasons why he was disgusted with wealth.

First, *we can't keep it* (Eccl. 2:18). The day would come when Solomon would die and leave everything to his successor. This reminds us of our Lord's warning in the parable of the rich fool (Luke 12:13–21) and Paul's words in 1 Timothy 6:7–10. A Jewish proverb says, "There are no pockets in shrouds."

Second, *we can't protect it* (Eccl. 2:19–20). It's bad enough that we must leave our wealth behind, but even worse that we might leave it to somebody who will waste it! Suppose he or she is a fool and tears down everything we have built up? Solomon didn't know it at the time, but his son Rehoboam would do that very thing (1 Kings 11:41—12:24).

Third, *we can't enjoy it as we should* (Eccl. 2:21–23). If all we do is think about our wealth and worry about what will happen to it, we will make our lives miserable. We do all the work and then leave the wealth to somebody who didn't even work for it (v. 21). Is that fair? We spend days in travail and grief and have many sleepless nights,

> yet our heirs never experience any of this. It all seems so futile. "What does a man get for all the toil and anxious striving with which he labors under the sun?" (v. 22 NIV).
>
> —*Be Satisfied*, pages 44–45

8. Review the three reasons Solomon was disgusted with wealth. What do these reasons tell us about him? About the pursuit of money as a life goal? How is this still true today?

More to Consider: We are stewards of our wealth; God is the Provider (Deut. 8:18) and the Owner, and we have the privilege of enjoying it and using it for His glory. How does Matthew 6:19–34 answer the question "If we can't take it with us, what's the point of wealth?"

From the Commentary

> Ecclesiastes 2:24–26 is the first of six "conclusions" in the book, each of which emphasizes the importance of accepting life as God's gift and enjoying it in God's will

(3:12–15, 22; 5:18–20; 8:15; 9:7–10; 11:9–10). Solomon is not advocating "Eat, drink and be merry, for tomorrow we die!" That is the philosophy of fatalism, not faith. Rather, he is saying, "Thank God for what you do have, and enjoy it to the glory of God." Paul gave his approval to this attitude when he exhorted us to trust "in the living God, who gives us richly all things to enjoy" (1 Tim. 6:17 NKJV).

Solomon made it clear that not only were the blessings from God, but even the *enjoyment of the blessings* was God's gift to us (Eccl. 2:24). He considered it "evil" if a person had all the blessings of life from God but could not enjoy them (6:1–5). It is easy to see why the Jewish people read Ecclesiastes at the Feast of Tabernacles, for Tabernacles is their great time of thanksgiving and rejoicing for God's abundant provision of their needs.

—*Be Satisfied*, page 46

9. Why do people often quote the "eat, drink, and be merry" verse as a life motto? What does it mean that the blessings we experience are from God? How does that change our views about enjoying life? How can the "eat, drink, and be merry" verse be reframed to celebrate God's provision? Rewrite it with that in mind.

From the Commentary

This completes the first section of Ecclesiastes—*The Problem Declared.* Solomon has presented four arguments that seem to prove that life is really not worth living: the monotony of life (Eccl. 1:4–11), the vanity of wisdom (1:12–18), the futility of wealth (2:1–11), and the certainty of death (2:12–23). His argument appears to be true *if* you look at life "under the sun," that is, only from the human point of view.

But when you bring God into the picture, everything changes! (Note that God is not mentioned from 1:14 to 2:23.) Life and death, wisdom and wealth, are all in His hands; He wants us to enjoy His blessings and please His heart. If we rejoice in the gifts but forget the Giver, then we are ungrateful idolaters.

In the next eight chapters, Solomon will consider each of these four arguments and refute them.

—*Be Satisfied*, page 47

10. Why did Solomon present the negative arguments before refuting them? Why wouldn't he just present the positive evidence?

Looking Inward

Take a moment to reflect on all that you've explored thus far in this study of Ecclesiastes 2. Review your notes and answers and think about how each of these things matters in your life today.

Tips for Small Groups: To get the most out of this section, form pairs or trios and have group members take turns answering these questions. Be honest and as open as you can in this discussion, but most of all, be encouraging and supportive of others. Be sensitive to those who are going through particularly difficult times and don't press for people to speak if they're uncomfortable doing so.

11. What are some of the more ridiculous things you've done to find meaning and purpose in life? What led to those choices? What was the result of those pursuits? How do you view those now, upon reflection?

12. What are some things in your life that lead you to think about big questions like what life means and what really matters? What prompts contemplation of the end of life? What does this tell you about your faith life? About your current relationship with God?

13. Have you ever made the pursuit of wealth a life goal? If so, why? How did that work out? Or, if you're still pursuing wealth, how is it going now? Where does your faith intersect with the goal of pursuing wealth?

Going Forward

14. Think of one or two things that you have learned that you'd like to work on in the coming week. Remember that this is all about quality, not quantity. It's better to work on one specific area of life and do it well than to work on many and do poorly (or to be so overwhelmed that you simply don't try).

Do you need to let go of selfish or unimportant pursuits? Do you need to cultivate gratitude for what you have? Be specific. Go back through Ecclesiastes 2 and put a star next to the phrase or verse that is most encouraging to you. Consider memorizing this verse.

Real-Life Application Ideas: Take a look at your monthly budget, or review your expenses in the past couple of months. What do the entries tell you about the things you prioritize? How much time and money do you spend on entertainment? On things that develop your character or faith? Talk with family members about your discoveries, then ask God for wisdom as you consider readjusting your priorities so they reflect the truth of your faith.

Seeking Help

15. Write a prayer below (or simply pray one in silence), inviting God to work on your mind and heart in those areas you've noted in the Going Forward section. Be honest about your desires and fears.

Notes for Small Groups:

- *Look for ways to put into practice the things you wrote in the Going Forward section. Talk with other group members about your ideas and commit to being accountable to one another.*
- *During the coming week, ask the Holy Spirit to continue to reveal truth to you from what you've read and studied.*
- *Before you start the next lesson, read Ecclesiastes 3. For more in-depth lesson preparation, read chapter 4, "Time and Toil," in* Be Satisfied.

Toil

(ECCLESIASTES 3)

Before you begin …

- *Pray for the Holy Spirit to reveal truth and wisdom as you go through this lesson.*
- *Read Ecclesiastes 3. This lesson references chapter 4 in* Be Satisfied. *It will be helpful for you to have your Bible and a copy of the commentary available as you work through this lesson.*

Getting Started

From the Commentary

Ponder these quotations from two famous professors: "Why shouldn't things be largely absurd, futile, and transitory? They are so, and we are so, and they and we go very well together." That's from philosopher George Santayana, who taught at Harvard from 1889 to 1912.

"There is no reason to suppose that a man's life has any more meaning than the life of the humblest insect that crawls from one annihilation to another." That was written by Joseph Wood Krutch, professor of English at Columbia University from 1937 to 1952.

Both of these men were brilliant in their fields, but most of us would not agree with what they wrote. We believe that something grander is involved in human life than mere transitory existence. We are *not* like insects. Surely Dr. Krutch knew that insects have *life cycles*, but men and women have *histories*. One bee is pretty much like another bee, but people are unique and no two stories are the same. You can write *The Life of the Bee*, but you can't write *The Life of the Man* or *The Life of the Woman*.

If we as individuals are not unique, then we are not important; if we are not important, then life has no meaning. If life has no meaning, life isn't worth living. We might as well follow the Epicurean philosophy: "Let us eat and drink, for tomorrow we die."

Solomon has presented four arguments proving that life was nothing but grasping broken soap bubbles and chasing after the wind. But he was too wise a man to let his own arguments go unchallenged, so in Ecclesiastes 3—10, he reexamined each of them carefully. His first argument was *the monotony of life* (1:4–11), and he examined it in Ecclesiastes 3:1—5:9.

—*Be Satisfied*, pages 51–52

1. Why did Solomon present four arguments about the futility of life, then immediately challenge his own arguments? What are the factors that Solomon said must be considered before you can label life as monotonous and meaningless?

2. Choose one verse or phrase from Ecclesiastes 3 that stands out to you. This could be something you're intrigued by, something that makes you uncomfortable, something that puzzles you, something that resonates with you, or just something you want to examine further. Write that here.

Going Deeper

From the Commentary

You don't have to be a philosopher or a scientist to know that "times and seasons" are a regular part of life, no

> matter where you live. Were it not for the dependability of God-ordained "natural laws," both science and daily life would be chaotic, if not impossible. Not only are there times and seasons in this world, but there is also an overruling providence in our lives. From before our birth to the moment of our death, God is accomplishing His divine purposes, even though we don't always understand what He is doing.
>
> In fourteen statements, Solomon affirmed that God is at work in our individual lives, seeking to accomplish His will. All of these events come from God, and they are good *in their time.*
>
> —*Be Satisfied*, page 52

3. Review Ecclesiastes 3:1–8. What are some of the ways Solomon affirmed that God is at work in our lives? What does it mean that an event is good "in its time"? What does this tell us about God's ways? About His will for our lives?

More to Consider: Read Psalm 139:13–16. How does this passage speak to the idea that God has prepared us individually for the work He has for us to do? (See Eph. 2:10.)

From the Commentary

> Being an agricultural people, the Jews appreciated the seasons. In fact, their religious calendar was based on the agricultural year (Lev. 23). Men may plow and sow, but only God can give the increase (Ps. 65:9–13). "Plucking" may refer either to reaping or to pulling up unproductive plants. A successful farmer knows that nature works for him only if he works with nature.
>
> Ecclesiastes 3:3 probably refers not to war (v. 8) or self-defense, but to the results of sickness and plague in the land (1 Sam. 2:6). God permits some to die, while others are healed. This does not imply that we should refuse medical aid, for God can use both means and miracles to accomplish His purposes (Isa. 38).
>
> —*Be Satisfied*, page 53

4. Review Ecclesiastes 3:2. What does this verse reveal about the secret to a successful life? What does 3:3 teach us about God's role in healing? About our responsibility to care for one another?

From Today's World

Ecclesiastes talks a lot about time—not just "a time for this" and "a time for that," but about the futility of trying to affect time. Solomon's examination of the temporary nature of our existence might have seemed a new idea in his day, but it's certainly nothing new today. The "live fast, die young" philosophy is a popular one, especially among the youth of today. Whether or not they actually subscribe to such a philosophy, it certainly does have an impact on the way people often prioritize their lives—making sure to have fun first and worry about responsibilities later.

5. What's so appealing about the "live fast, die young" philosophy? In what ways are people who subscribe to this way of life misinterpreting Solomon's words? What's the difference between "live fast, die young" and "live in the moment" philosophies? In what ways is the latter more compatible with God's will?

From the Commentary

> Tour guides in Israel will tell you that God gave stones to an angel and told him to distribute them across the world—and he tripped right over Palestine! It is indeed a rocky land, and farmers must clear their fields before they

can plow and plant. If you wanted to hurt an enemy, you filled up his field with stones (2 Kings 3:19, 25). People also gathered stones for building walls and houses. Stones are neither good nor bad; it all depends on what you do with them. If your enemy fills your land with rocks, don't throw them back. Build something out of them!

People in the Near East openly show their affections, kissing and hugging when they meet and when they part. So, you could paraphrase Ecclesiastes 3:5, "A time to say hello and a time to say good-bye." This might also refer to the relationship of a husband and wife (Lev. 15:19–31; see 1 Cor. 7:5).

—*Be Satisfied*, pages 53–54

6. Review Ecclesiastes 3:5. What does this verse tell us about God's relationship with His people? What is the time for gathering stones all about? What does the time to say "hello" and the time to say "good-bye" reveal about God's will for relationships?

From the Commentary

> In Ecclesiastes 3:9–14, the Preacher adjusted his sights and no longer looked at life *only* "under the sun." He brought God into the picture, and this gave him a new perspective. In verse 9, he repeated the opening question of 1:3: "Is all this labor really worth it?"
>
> In view of the travail that we experience from day to day, life may seem like a strange gift, but it is God's gift just the same. We "exercise" ourselves in trying to explain life's enigmas, but we don't always succeed. If we believingly accept life as a gift, and thank God for it, we will have a better attitude toward the burdens that come our way. If we grudgingly accept life as a burden, then we will miss the gifts that come our way.
>
> —*Be Satisfied*, page 55

7. What was Solomon's first answer to the question "Is life worth it?" (See Eccl. 3:10.) In what ways did Solomon see life as a gift? What's the spiritual truth of the statement "Outlook helps to determine outcome"?

From the Commentary

> The Preacher hinted that life can be enjoyable now in Ecclesiastes 2:24 and was careful to say that this enjoyment of life is the gift of God (see 3:13; 6:2; 1 Tim. 6:17). "The enjoyment of life" is an important theme in Ecclesiastes and is mentioned in each of the four sections of chapters 3—10. Solomon is encouraging not pagan hedonism, but rather the practice of enjoying God's gifts as the fruit of one's labor, no matter how difficult life may be. Life appears to be transitory, but whatever God does is forever, so when we live for Him and let Him have His way, life is meaningful and manageable. Instead of complaining about what we don't have, let's enjoy what we do have and thank God for it.
>
> —*Be Satisfied*, pages 55–56

8. Was Solomon saying "don't worry, be happy" in Ecclesiastes 3:12–14? Explain. What's the difference between faith in faith and faith in God? How does faith in God affect our enjoyment of life?

More to Consider: What does it mean to be a part of God's eternal plan? (See John 14:1–6; 2 Cor. 4.) How does being a part of this plan affect our enjoyment of life? Respond to this statement from the Puritan pastor Thomas Watson: "Eternity to the godly is a day that has no sunset; eternity to the wicked is a night that has no sunrise."

From the Commentary

> Solomon already mentioned the certainty of death in Ecclesiastes 2:12–23, and he will bring the subject up several times before he ends his book (4:8; 5:15–16; 6:6; 8:8; 9:2–3, 12; 12:7–8). Life, death, time, and eternity: these are the "ingredients" that make up our brief experience in this world, and they must not be ignored.
>
> Ecclesiastes 3:15 helps us recall 1:9–11 and gives us the assurance that God is in control of the "cycle of life." The past seems to repeat itself so that "there is no new thing under the sun" (1:9), but God can break into history and do what He pleases. His many miracles are evidence that the "cycle" is a pattern and not a prison.
>
> —*Be Satisfied*, pages 56–57

9. Review Ecclesiastes 3:15–22. What is the "vicious circle" that Solomon addressed in this passage? How did Jesus break that circle? What does this mean for those who follow Him? (See 2 Cor. 5:17–21.)

From the Commentary

The Bible says that death occurs when the spirit leaves the body (James 2:26; see Gen. 35:18; Luke 8:55). In Ecclesiastes 3:21, Solomon indicates that men and animals do not have the same experience at death, even though they both turn to dust after death. Man's spirit goes to God (see 12:7), while the spirit of a beast simply ceases to exist. You find a similar contrast expressed in Psalm 49.

The Preacher closed this section by reminding us again to accept life from God's hand and enjoy it while we can (Eccl. 3:22). Nobody knows what the future holds; and even if we did know, we can't return to life after we have died and start to enjoy it again (see 6:12; 7:14; 9:3). Knowing that God is in sovereign control of life (3:1), we can submit to Him and be at peace.

Faith learns to live with seeming inconsistencies and absurdities, for we live by promises and not by explanations. We can't explain life, but we must experience life, either enduring it or enjoying it.

—*Be Satisfied*, pages 58–59

10. In what ways did Solomon call us to accept life? What does it look like to be satisfied with what God gives to us in this life? How does growing in character and godliness help us live the truth of Philippians 4:11—"to be content whatever the circumstances"?

Looking Inward

Take a moment to reflect on all that you've explored thus far in this study of Ecclesiastes 3. Review your notes and answers and think about how each of these things matters in your life today.

Tips for Small Groups: To get the most out of this section, form pairs or trios and have group members take turns answering these questions. Be honest and as open as you can in this discussion, but most of all, be encouraging and supportive of others. Be sensitive to those who are going through particularly difficult times and don't press for people to speak if they're uncomfortable doing so.

11. Which of the "times and seasons" described in Ecclesiastes 3 are you experiencing now? How are you dealing with the challenges? How does knowing that there is a "time for everything" help you through both the good and bad times?

12. What are some ways you've tried to find meaning through enjoyment of life? What are some ways God gives you enjoyment in your life? In what places in your life is your will at odds with God's will? How does that affect your enjoyment of life?

13. When have you witnessed or experienced God's ability to break into the cycle of life and effect some change? How does this encourage you? What does it say about God's care and concern for His people? For you in particular?

Going Forward

14. Think of one or two things that you have learned that you'd like to work on in the coming week. Remember that this is all about quality, not quantity. It's better to work on one specific area of life and do it well than to work on many and do poorly (or to be so overwhelmed that you simply don't try).

Do you need to learn more about what it means to truly enjoy the life God has given you? Be specific. Go back through Ecclesiastes 3 and put a star next to the phrase or verse that is most encouraging to you. Consider memorizing this verse.

Real-Life Application Ideas: It's easy to get caught up in the challenges we're facing. Sometimes it's good to step back from the hardship and look for clues about how God is providing, about where God is showing Himself to us and telling us He loves us. Take this week to look for clues that reveal God's presence in your life. Be open to surprising moments when you find enjoyment in God's will. Don't ignore the challenges you're facing. Instead, release them to God and trust that He will take care of them. And as you do, delight in the fact that God truly does love you. That's a kind of enjoyment you can find in the midst of all circumstances.

Seeking Help

15. Write a prayer below (or simply pray one in silence), inviting God to work on your mind and heart in those areas you've noted in the Going Forward section. Be honest about your desires and fears.

Notes for Small Groups:

- *Look for ways to put into practice the things you wrote in the Going Forward section. Talk with other group members about your ideas and commit to being accountable to one another.*
- *During the coming week, ask the Holy Spirit to continue to reveal truth to you from what you've read and studied.*
- *Before you start the next lesson, read Ecclesiastes 4—5. For more in-depth lesson preparation, read chapters 5 and 6, "Life Just Isn't Fair" and "Stop, Thief!," in* Be Satisfied.

It Isn't Fair

(ECCLESIASTES 4—5)

Before you begin …

- *Pray for the Holy Spirit to reveal truth and wisdom as you go through this lesson.*
- *Read Ecclesiastes 4—5. This lesson references chapters 5 and 6 in* Be Satisfied. *It will be helpful for you to have your Bible and a copy of the commentary available as you work through this lesson.*

Getting Started

From the Commentary

When Solomon first examined life "under the sun," his viewpoint was detached and philosophical (Eccl. 1:4–11). His conclusion was that life was meaningless and monotonous. But when he examined the question again, he went to where people really lived and discovered that life was not that simple. As he observed real people in real situations, the king had to deal with some painful facts, like life and death, time and eternity, and the final judgment.

> Phillips Brooks, Anglican Bishop of Massachusetts a century ago, told ministerial students to read three "books": the Book of books, the Bible; the book of nature; and the book of mankind. The ivory tower investigator will never have a balanced view of his subject if he remains in his ivory tower. Learning and living must be brought together.
>
> In Ecclesiastes 4, Solomon recorded his observations from visiting four different places and watching several people go through a variety of experiences.
>
> —*Be Satisfied*, page 63

1. Why did Solomon choose to observe people in real life as he continued to explore the meaning of existence? What did he learn from this new perspective? How does the message of Proverbs 27:1 relate to these conclusions?

2. Choose one verse or phrase from Ecclesiastes 4—5 that stands out to you. This could be something you're intrigued by, something that makes you uncomfortable, something that puzzles you, something that resonates with you, or just something you want to examine further. Write that here.

Going Deeper

From the Commentary

> "Politics" has been defined as "the conduct of public affairs for private advantage." The nation of Israel had an adequate judicial system (Ex. 18:13–27; Deut. 17; 19), based on divine law; but the system could be corrupted just like anything else (Eccl. 5:8). Moses warned officials to judge honestly and fairly (Lev. 19:15; Deut. 1:17), and both the prophet and the psalmist lashed out against social injustice (Ps. 82; Isa. 56:1; 59:1ff.; Amos 1—2). Solomon had been a wise and just king (1 Kings 3:16–28), but it was impossible for him to guarantee the integrity of every officer in his government.
>
> —*Be Satisfied*, page 64

3. What did Solomon observe in the courtroom in Ecclesiastes 4? What did this observation teach him about oppression? How does this play into his examination of the meaning of life?

More to Consider: Read 1 Timothy 2:1–6. What do these verses tell us about how we are to respond to authority? Why is this significant to Solomon's story? Why is it important in ours?

From the Commentary

Disgusted with what he saw in the "halls of justice," the king went down to the marketplace to watch the various laborers at work. Surely he would not be disappointed there, for honest toil is a gift from God. Even Adam had work to do in the Garden (Gen. 2:15), and our Lord was a carpenter when He was here on earth (Mark 6:3). Solomon considered four different kinds of men. The first two were the industrious man and the idle man.

It was natural for Solomon first to find a laborer who was working hard. For, after all, had not the king extolled the virtues of hard work in the book of Proverbs? The man was not only busy, but he was skillful in his work and competent in all he did. He had mastered the techniques of his trade.

Solomon moved from one extreme to the other and began to study a man who had no ambition at all. Perhaps the king could learn about life by examining the antithesis, the way scientists study cold to better understand heat.

—*Be Satisfied*, pages 65–66

4. Review Ecclesiastes 4:4–6. What did Solomon learn from observing both the industrious man and the lazy man? Why might it have been particularly difficult for him to watch the idle man? (See Prov. 18:9; 19:15; 24:30–34.)

From the Commentary

> The third man Solomon observed, the integrated man, was a man whose life was balanced: He was productive in his work, but he was also careful to take time for quietness. He did not run in the rat race, but neither did he try to run away from the normal responsibilities of life. A 1989 Harris survey revealed that the amount of leisure time enjoyed by the average American had shrunk 37 percent from 1973. This suggests that fewer people know how to keep life in balance. They are caught in the rat race and don't know how to escape.
>
> Finally, Solomon noticed a solitary man—an independent man—very hard at work, so he went to question him. The king discovered that the man had no relatives or partners to help him in his business, nor did he desire any help. He wanted all the profit for himself. But he was so busy, he

> had no time to enjoy his profits. And if he died, he had no family to inherit his wealth. In other words, all his labor was in vain.
>
> —*Be Satisfied*, pages 66–67

5. What did Solomon learn from the integrated man? The independent man? Which sort of person is most common in today's society? What might Solomon say about them?

From the Commentary

> Solomon's experience with the independent man caused him to consider the importance of friendship and the value of people doing things together. He may have recalled the Jewish proverb, "A friendless man is like a left hand bereft of the right." Perhaps he watched some pilgrims on the highway and drew the conclusion, "Two are better than one."
>
> Two are certainly better than one when it comes to *working* (Eccl. 4:9) because two workers can get more done. Even when they divide the profits, they still get a better

return for their efforts than if they had worked alone. Also, it's much easier to do difficult jobs together because one can be an encouragement to the other.

Two are better when it comes to *walking* (Eccl. 4:10). Roads and paths in Palestine were not paved or even leveled, and there were many hidden rocks in the fields. It was not uncommon for even the most experienced traveler to stumble and fall, perhaps break a bone, or even fall into a hidden pit (Ex. 21:33–34). How wonderful to have a friend who can help you up (or out). But if this applies to our *physical* falls, how much more does it apply to those times when we stumble in our *spiritual* walk and need restoration (Gal. 6:1–2)? How grateful we should be for Christian friends who help us walk straight.

—*Be Satisfied*, page 68

6. Review Ecclesiastes 4:9–12. What does this (and the rest of this chapter) teach about the importance of community? Of friendship? What does it say about the importance of balance in life? How do we find that balance?

From the Commentary

> Solomon had visited the courtroom, the marketplace, the highway, and the palace. Now he paid a visit to the temple, that magnificent building whose construction he had supervised. He watched the worshippers come and go, praising God, praying, sacrificing, and making vows. He noted that many of them were not at all sincere in their worship, and they left the sacred precincts in worse spiritual condition than when they had entered. What was their sin? They were robbing God of the reverence and honor that He deserved. Their acts of worship were perfunctory, insincere, and hypocritical.
>
> In today's language, "Keep thy foot!" means "Watch your step!" Even though God's glorious presence doesn't dwell in our church buildings as it did in the temple, believers today still need to heed this warning. *The worship of God is the highest ministry of the church and must come from devoted hearts and yielded wills.*
>
> —*Be Satisfied*, pages 75–76

7. Review Ecclesiastes 5:1–7. What was most surprising about Solomon's visit to the temple? What warnings does this give us for the church today? Why is it so wrong for people to worship while harboring unconfessed sins? (See Isa. 1:10–20; Amos 5; Ps. 50.)

From the Commentary

> Prayer is serious business. Like marriage, "it must not be entered into lightly or carelessly, but soberly and in the fear of God." If you and I were privileged to bring our needs and requests to the White House or to Buckingham Palace, we would prepare our words carefully and exhibit proper behavior. How much more important it is when we come to the throne of Almighty God? Yet, there is so much flippant praying done by people who seem to know nothing about the fear of the Lord.
>
> Ecclesiastes 5:3 presents an analogy: Just as many dreams show that the person sleeping is a hard worker, so many words show that the person praying is a fool (Prov. 29:20). I recall a church prayer meeting during which a young man prayed eloquently and at great length, but nobody sensed the power of God at work. When an uneducated immigrant stood up and stammered out her brief prayer in broken English, we all said a fervent "Amen!" We sensed that God had heard her requests. Spurgeon said, "It is not the length of our prayers, but the strength of our prayers, that makes the difference."
>
> —*Be Satisfied*, pages 76–77

8. Read Psalm 141:1–2 and Matthew 6:7; 12:34–37. How do these verses address Solomon's observations about prayer? Why is sincere prayer such an important part of a faith life? How do we pursue an authentic prayer life?

More to Consider: Read Numbers 30; Deuteronomy 23:21–23; and Acts 18:18. What do these passages teach about the opportunity to express devotion to God? How is this different from being required to make vows in order to be accepted by God? Why is this distinction important?

From the Commentary

> Solomon left the temple and went to the city hall, where he again witnessed corrupt politicians oppressing the poor (Eccl. 3:16–17; 4:1–3). The government officials violated the law by using their authority to help themselves and not to serve others, a practice condemned by Moses (Lev. 19:15; Deut. 24:17).
>
> The *New International Version* translation of Ecclesiastes 5:8 gives a vivid description of the situation: "One official is eyed by a higher one, and over them both are others higher still." Instead of the poor man getting a fair hearing, "the matter is lost in red tape and bureaucracy" (v. 8 TLB), and the various officials pocket the money that should have gone to the innocent poor man.
>
> —*Be Satisfied*, pages 78–79

9. Why do you think Solomon wasn't surprised by the corruption he found? How is what Solomon found similar to what's happening in today's world? What was Solomon's response to the corruption? What do you think he would say about the corruption that's going on in today's world (even in the church)?

From the Commentary

Solomon had already discussed "the futility of wealth" in Ecclesiastes 2:1–11, and some of those ideas are repeated in 5:10–20. What he did in this section was demolish several of the myths that people hold about wealth. Because they hold to these illusions, they rob themselves of the blessings God has for them.

Some people treat money as though it were a god. They love it, make sacrifices for it, and think that it can do anything. Their minds are filled with thoughts about it; their lives are controlled by getting it and guarding it; and when they have it, they experience a great sense of security. What faith in the Lord does for the Christian, money does for many unbelievers. How often we hear people say, "Well, money may not be the number one thing in life, but it's way ahead of whatever is number two!"

The person who loves money cannot be satisfied no matter how much is in the bank account—because the human heart was made to be satisfied only by God (3:11). "Take heed and beware of covetousness," warned Jesus, "for one's life does not consist in the abundance of the things which he possesses" (Luke 12:15 NKJV). First the person loves money, and then he loves *more* money, and the disappointing pursuit has begun that can lead to all sorts of problems. "For the love of money is a root of all kinds of evil" (1 Tim. 6:10 NKJV).

—*Be Satisfied*, pages 79–80

10. What myths did Solomon destroy in Ecclesiastes 5:10–20? How do these myths appear in modern society? How does believing these myths rob people of God's blessings?

Looking Inward

Take a moment to reflect on all that you've explored thus far in this study of Ecclesiastes 4—5. Review your notes and answers and think about how each of these things matters in your life today.

> *Tips for Small Groups: To get the most out of this section, form pairs or trios and have group members take turns answering these questions. Be honest and as open as you can in this discussion, but most of all, be encouraging and supportive of others. Be sensitive to those who are going through particularly difficult times and don't press for people to speak if they're uncomfortable doing so.*

11. What type of person are you: industrious, idle, integrated, or independent? What type would you like to be? What makes it difficult for you to be that person? How is your faith affected by the type of person you are?

12. What are some of the ways you find balance in life? What are the challenges to maintaining a healthy balance? How does your faith in God help you with that balancing act?

13. What is your perspective on prayer? What does "sincere prayer" look like in your life? Why is prayer important to you?

Going Forward

14. Think of one or two things that you have learned that you'd like to work on in the coming week. Remember that this is all about quality, not quantity. It's better to work on one specific area of life and do it well than to work on many and do poorly (or to be so overwhelmed that you simply don't try).

Do you need to find balance? Be specific. Go back through Ecclesiastes 4—5 and put a star next to the phrase or verse that is most encouraging to you. Consider memorizing this verse.

Real-Life Application Ideas: You've already considered your budget and priorities; now take a close look solely at how you deal with money. Look for areas where your actions with money are at odds with God's will. If you're too focused on gaining money or possessions and not focused enough on trusting God, consider practical solutions to that imbalance (such as donating money to good causes, spending less on selfish pursuits, using some of your money to build your character or faith life).

Seeking Help

15. Write a prayer below (or simply pray one in silence), inviting God to work on your mind and heart in those areas you've noted in the Going Forward section. Be honest about your desires and fears.

Notes for Small Groups:

- *Look for ways to put into practice the things you wrote in the Going Forward section. Talk with other group members about your ideas and commit to being accountable to one another.*
- *During the coming week, ask the Holy Spirit to continue to reveal truth to you from what you've read and studied.*
- *Before you start the next lesson, read Ecclesiastes 6. For more in-depth lesson preparation, read chapter 7, "Is Life a Dead-End Street?," in* Be Satisfied.

Dead End?
(ECCLESIASTES 6)

Before you begin …

- *Pray for the Holy Spirit to reveal truth and wisdom as you go through this lesson.*
- *Read Ecclesiastes 6. This lesson references chapter 7 in* Be Satisfied. *It will be helpful for you to have your Bible and a copy of the commentary available as you work through this lesson.*

Getting Started

From the Commentary

Is life a dead-end street? Sometimes it seems to be, especially when we don't reach our goals or when we reach our goals but don't feel fulfilled in our achievement. More than one person in the Bible became so discouraged with life that he either wanted to die or wished he had never been born.

Perhaps the basic problem is that life confronts us with too

> many mysteries we can't fathom and too many puzzles we can't solve. For life to be truly satisfying, it has to make sense. When it doesn't make sense, we get frustrated. If people can't see a purpose in life, especially when they go through deep suffering, they start to question God and even wonder if life is worthwhile.
>
> —*Be Satisfied*, page 88

1. Read about these biblical characters who at one time wanted to die or wished they'd never been born: Moses (Num. 11:15), Elijah (1 Kings 19:4), Job (Job 3:21; 7:15), Jeremiah (Jer. 8:3; 15:10), Jonah (Jonah 4:3), and Paul (2 Cor. 1:8–11). What led to each of these people's struggle? How were their struggles similar to what Solomon was exploring in Ecclesiastes 6?

2. Choose one verse or phrase from Ecclesiastes 6 that stands out to you. This could be something you're intrigued by, something that makes you uncomfortable, something that puzzles you, something that resonates with you, or just something you want to examine further. Write that here.

Going Deeper

From the Commentary

> What a seeming tragedy it is to have all the resources for a satisfying life and yet not be able to enjoy them for one reason or another. More than one person has worked hard and looked forward to a comfortable retirement only to have a heart attack and become either an invalid or a statistic. Or perhaps the peace of retirement is shattered by a crisis in the family that begins to drain both money and strength. Why do these things happen?
>
> Solomon mentioned this subject in Ecclesiastes 5:19 and hinted at it in 3:13. To him, it was a basic principle that nobody can truly enjoy the gifts of God apart from the God who gives the gifts.
>
> —*Be Satisfied*, page 88

3. Review Ecclesiastes 6:1–6. Why is it impossible to enjoy the gifts of God apart from God? What does it look like to attempt this? How is this idolatry? How is enjoyment with God different from enjoyment apart from God?

From the Commentary

Ecclesiastes 6:3–6 surely deals with a hypothetical case, because nobody lives for two thousand years, and no monogamous marriage is likely to produce a hundred children. (Solomon's son Rehoboam had eighty-eight children, but he had eighteen wives and sixty concubines—like father, like son. See 2 Chron. 11:21.) The Preacher was obviously exaggerating here in order to make his point: No matter how much you possess, if you don't possess the power to enjoy it, you might just as well never have been born.

Here is a man with abundant resources and a large family, both of which, to an Old Testament Jew, were marks of God's special favor. But his family does not love him, for when he died, he was not lamented. That's the meaning of "he has no burial" (see Jer. 22:18–19). His relatives stayed around him only to use his money (5:11), and they wondered when the old man would die. When he finally did die, his surviving relatives could hardly wait for the reading of the will.

The rich man was really poor. For some reason, perhaps sickness, he couldn't enjoy his money. And he couldn't enjoy his large family because there was no love in the home. They didn't even weep when the man died.

"I have learned, in whatsoever state I am, therewith to be content," Paul wrote to the Philippians (4:11). The Greek word *autarkes*, translated "content," carries the idea of "self-contained, adequate, needing nothing from the outside."

—*Be Satisfied*, pages 89–90

4. What was Solomon's conclusion about the rich man? Where does the ability to enjoy life come from? Where do we find contentment? Where do we find the resources to maintain contentment in trying times? (See Phil. 4:13.)

From Today's World

The suicide rate in America is higher than it's ever been. The Internet Age has brought out all kinds of new challenges for young and old people alike. Kids are bullied for their beliefs. Media preaches a beauty standard that few can live up to. The pursuit of meaning is often thwarted by a society that isn't shy about acknowledging (in movies and television) that futility is a reality we all must somehow face.

5. Why do so many people give in to a sense of futility and take their lives? How does Solomon's book speak to this futility? What might he say to those who feel lost and purposeless? What can we do as a church to help people overcome the feelings of futility?

From the Commentary

> Solomon had spoken about the rich man; now in Ecclesiastes 6:7–9 he discusses the situation of the poor man. Rich and poor alike labor to stay alive. We must either produce food or earn money to buy it. The rich man can let his money work for him, but the poor man has to use his muscles if he and his family are going to eat. But even after all this labor, the appetite of neither one is fully satisfied.
>
> Why does a person eat? So that he can add years to his life. But what good is it for me to add years to my life *if I don't add life to my years*? I'm like the birds that I watch in the backyard. They spend all their waking hours either looking for food or escaping from enemies. (We have cats in our neighborhood.) These birds are not really *living*; they are only *existing*. Yet they are fulfilling the purposes for which the Creator made them—and they even sing about it!
>
> —*Be Satisfied*, page 91

6. How would Solomon propose we add life to our years instead of merely years to our lives? What is the message here for those who are poor? How does this message relate to modern society and its many challenges?

From the Commentary

> A century ago, when the United States was starting to experience prosperity and expansion, the American naturalist Henry David Thoreau warned that men were devising "improved means to unimproved ends." He should see our world today. We can send messages around the world in seconds, but do we have anything significant to say? We can transmit pictures even from the moon, but our TV screens are stained with violence, sex, cheap advertising, and even cheaper entertainment.
>
> Ecclesiastes 6:9 is Solomon's version of the familiar saying, "A bird in the hand is worth two in the bush." This proverb has been around for a long time. The Greek biographer Plutarch (AD 46–120) wrote, "He is a fool who lets slip a bird in the hand for a bird in the bush." Solomon is saying, "It's better to have little and really enjoy it than to dream about much and never attain it."
>
> —*Be Satisfied*, pages 91–92

7. Was Solomon saying that it's wrong to dream great dreams or to have a burning ambition to accomplish something in life? Explain. What are the circumstances that turn dreams into nightmares in life? What was Solomon's answer to this dilemma?

From the Commentary

> Thus far, Solomon has said that life is a dead-end street for two kinds of people: those who have riches but no enjoyment and those who labor but have no satisfaction. But he has tried to point out that true happiness is not the automatic result of making a good living; it is the blessed by-product of making a good life. If you devote your life only to the pursuit of happiness, you will be miserable; however, if you devote your life to doing God's will, you will find happiness as well.
>
> The Preacher was not finished. He knew that life was also a dead-end street for a third kind of person—the person who required answers to all of life's questions. Solomon was not condemning honest inquiry, because Ecclesiastes is the record of his own investigation into the meaning of life. Rather, Solomon was saying, "There are some questions about life that nobody can answer. But our ignorance must not be used as an excuse for skepticism or unbelief."
>
> —*Be Satisfied*, pages 92–93

8. Review Ecclesiastes 6:10–12. Why is it futile to seek answers to all of life's questions? What's wrong with making the pursuit of knowledge a life goal? How do we find balance in this area of life? How might our ignorance actually point us toward God instead of away from Him?

More to Consider: To the Jewish mind, giving a name to something is the same as fixing its character and stating what the thing really is. During creation, God named the things that He made, and nobody changed those designations. "Light" is "light" and not "darkness"; "day" is "day" and not "night." (See Isa. 5:20.) What does our name "man" (Adam) mean? (See Gen. 2:7; 3:19.) What does this name tell us about God's purpose for us? How does this line up with Solomon's thoughts on the meaning of life in Ecclesiastes?

From the Commentary

> "Neither may he contend with him that is mightier than he" (Eccl. 6:10b). The word translated "contend" also means "dispute." Solomon seems to say, "It just doesn't pay to argue with God or to fight God. This is the way life is, so just accept it and let God have His way. You can't win, and even if you think you win, you ultimately lose."
>
> But this is a negative view of the will of God. It gives the impression that God's will is a difficult and painful thing that should be avoided at all cost. Jesus said that God's will was the food that nourished and satisfied Him (John 4:32–34). It was meat, not medicine. The will of God comes from the heart of God and is an expression of the love of God (see Ps. 33:11). What God wills for us is best for us, because He knows far more about us than we do.
>
> —*Be Satisfied*, pages 94–95

9. Why would anyone want to have his or her own way just for the privilege of exercising freedom? Why doesn't it pay to argue with God? How can insisting on having our own way become a kind of bondage? (See Rom. 1:24, 26, 28.)

From the Commentary

> In spite of what the astrologers, prophets, and fortune-tellers claim, nobody knows the future except God. It is futile to speculate. God gives us enough information to encourage us, but He does not cater to idle curiosity. One thing is sure: Death is coming, and we had better make the best use of our present opportunities. That is one of the major themes in Ecclesiastes.
>
> —*Be Satisfied*, pages 95–96

10. Why is it futile to speculate about the future? How is that different from preparing for the future? What does it look like in daily life to make the best of our present circumstances?

Looking Inward

Take a moment to reflect on all that you've explored thus far in this study of Ecclesiastes 6. Review your notes and answers and think about how each of these things matters in your life today.

> *Tips for Small Groups: To get the most out of this section, form pairs or trios and have group members take turns answering these questions. Be honest and as open as you can in this discussion, but most of all, be encouraging and supportive of others. Be sensitive to those who are going through particularly difficult times and don't press for people to speak if they're uncomfortable doing so.*

11. Are you more like Solomon's rich man, or the man who works hard but without satisfaction? Explain. What would Solomon tell you about your current relationship with wealth or the lack of it?

12. What are some of life's questions you wish you could answer? Would you be happy if you could answer all of the difficult questions? Why or why not? What would your faith life look like if you had all the answers? How does not knowing help you grow closer to God?

13. What are some ways you make the best of present circumstances? How does this help you to keep from fretting about the future? Would you want to know what the future holds for your life? Why or why not?

Going Forward

14. Think of one or two things that you have learned that you'd like to work on in the coming week. Remember that this is all about quality, not quantity. It's better to work on one specific area of life and do it well than to work on many and do poorly (or to be so overwhelmed that you simply don't try).

Do you need to stop pursuing wealth for wealth's sake? Be specific. Go back through Ecclesiastes 6 and put a star next to the phrase or verse that is most encouraging to you. Consider memorizing this verse.

Real-Life Application Ideas: Solomon wrote that it is better to have little and enjoy it than to dream about much and never attain it. This week, spend some time reflecting on all the "little" things God has blessed you with. Find ways to enjoy each of these things—whether it's a place to live, or a meal on your table, or the fact that you can express your faith freely. Think about how big each of these little things really is.

Seeking Help

15. Write a prayer below (or simply pray one in silence), inviting God to work on your mind and heart in those areas you've noted in the Going Forward section. Be honest about your desires and fears.

Notes for Small Groups:

- *Look for ways to put into practice the things you wrote in the Going Forward section. Talk with other group members about your ideas and commit to being accountable to one another.*
- *During the coming week, ask the Holy Spirit to continue to reveal truth to you from what you've read and studied.*
- *Before you start the next lesson, read Ecclesiastes 7—8. For more in-depth lesson preparation, read chapters 8 and 9, "How to Be Better Off" and "What About the Wicked?," in* Be Satisfied.

Better Off
(ECCLESIASTES 7—8)

Before you begin …

- *Pray for the Holy Spirit to reveal truth and wisdom as you go through this lesson.*
- *Read Ecclesiastes 7—8. This lesson references chapters 8 and 9 in* Be Satisfied. *It will be helpful for you to have your Bible and a copy of the commentary available as you work through this lesson.*

Getting Started

From the Commentary

"Better" is a key word in this chapter; Solomon used it at least eleven times. His listeners must have been shocked when they heard Solomon describe the "better things" that come to the life of the person who follows God's wisdom.

If given the choice, most people would rather go to a birthday party than to a funeral, but Solomon advised

> against it. Why? Because sorrow can do more good for the heart than laughter can. (The word *heart* is used four times in Ecclesiastes 7:1–4.) Solomon was certainly not a morose man with a gloomy lifestyle. After all, it was King Solomon who wrote Proverbs 15:13, 15; 17:22—and the Song of Solomon! Laughter can be like medicine that heals the broken heart, but sorrow can be like nourishing food that strengthens the inner person. It takes both for a balanced life, but few people realize this. There is "a time to laugh" (Eccl. 3:4).
>
> —*Be Satisfied*, page 100

1. According to Solomon, how can sorrow be good for a heart? Why does modern society tend to ignore the benefits of sorrow?

2. Choose one verse or phrase from Ecclesiastes 7—8 that stands out to you. This could be something you're intrigued by, something that makes you uncomfortable, something that puzzles you, something that resonates with you, or just something you want to examine further. Write that here.

Going Deeper

From the Commentary

> King Solomon compared the praise of fools to the burning thorns in a campfire: You hear a lot of noise, but you don't get much lasting good. (Again, Solomon used a play on words. In the Hebrew, "song" is *shir*, "pot" is *sir*, and "thorns" is *sirim*.) If we allow it, a wise person's rebuke will accomplish far more in our lives than will the flattery of fools. Solomon may have learned this truth from his father (Ps. 141:5), and he certainly emphasized it when he wrote the book of Proverbs (10:17; 12:1; 15:5; 17:10; 25:12; 27:5, 17; 29:1, 15).
>
> —*Be Satisfied*, page 102

3. Read some of the verses from Proverbs listed in the previous commentary excerpt. How can the "praise of fools" do harm to us? Where do we turn to find wise rebuke instead? What does modern society celebrate more, the praise of fools or wise rebuke? Explain.

From the Commentary

Beware of "easy" routes; they often become expensive detours that are difficult and painful. In 1976, my wife and I were driving through Scotland and a friend mapped out a "faster" route from Balmoral Castle to Inverness. It turned out to be a hazardous one-lane road that the local people called "The Devil's Elbow," and en route we met a bus and a cement truck! "Watch and pray" was our verse for that day.

Bribery appears to be a quick way to get things done (Eccl. 7:7), but it only turns a wise man into a fool and encourages the corruption already in the human heart. Far better that we wait patiently and humbly for God to work out His will than that we get angry and demand our own way (v. 8; see also Prov. 14:17; 16:32; James 1:19.)

"Better is the end of a thing than the beginning" applies when we are living according to God's wisdom. The beginning of sin leads to a terrible end—death (James 1:13–15)—but if God is at the beginning of what we do, He will see to it that we reach the ending successfully (Phil. 1:6; Heb. 12:2). The Christian believer can claim Romans 8:28 because he knows that God is at work in the world, accomplishing His purposes.

—*Be Satisfied*, page 103

4. In what ways is our culture today a "shortcut" society? Why are shortcuts so tempting in life? What is Solomon's caution about "the easy way"? What can we learn by trusting God in the long, difficult routes of life?

From the Commentary

> One of the marks of maturity is the ability to look at life in perspective and not get out of balance. When you have God's wisdom, you will be able to accept and deal with the changing experiences of life.
>
> Wisdom is better than a generous inheritance. Money can lose its value, or be stolen, but true wisdom keeps its value and cannot be lost, unless we become fools and abandon it deliberately. The person who has wealth but lacks wisdom will only waste his fortune, but the person who has wisdom will know how to get and use wealth. We should be grateful for the rich treasure of wisdom we have inherited from the past, and we should be ashamed of ourselves that we too often ignore it or disobey it.
>
> —*Be Satisfied*, page 104

5. Review Ecclesiastes 7:11–12. What are some ways wisdom is better than wealth? How is wisdom a better shelter than money? What message does today's world (inside and outside of the church) preach more readily: wisdom or wealth? What does that say about society? How should the church respond to that message?

From the Commentary

> Wisdom gives us perspective so that we aren't discouraged when times are difficult or arrogant when things are going well. It takes a good deal of spirituality to be able to accept prosperity as well as adversity, for often prosperity does greater damage (Phil. 4:10–13). Job reminded his wife of this truth when she told him to curse God and die: "What? Shall we receive good at the hand of God, and shall we not receive evil [trouble]?" (2:10). Earlier, Job had said, "The LORD gave, and the LORD hath taken away; blessed be the name of the LORD" (1:21).
>
> —*Be Satisfied*, page 105

6. How does God balance our lives with blessings and burdens? What would life be like if all we had were blessings? Burdens? How does God turn one into the other in order to keep us focused on Him?

From the Commentary

"Wisdom makes one wise man more powerful than ten rulers in a city" (Eccl. 7:19 NIV). The wise person fears the Lord and therefore does not fear anyone or anything else (Ps. 112). He walks with the Lord and has the adequacy necessary to face the challenges of life, including war (see Eccl. 9:13–18). What are some of the problems in life that we must face and overcome?

Sin (Eccl. 7:20; note 1 Kings 8:46). We are all guilty of both sins of omission ("doeth good") and sins of commission ("sinneth not"). If we walk in the fear of God and follow His wisdom, we will be able to detect and defeat the wicked one when he comes to tempt us. Wisdom will guide us and guard us in our daily walk.

What people say about us (Eccl. 7:21–22). The wise person pays no attention to the gossip of the day because he has more important matters to attend to. Charles Spurgeon told his pastoral students that the minister ought to have one blind eye and one deaf ear. "You cannot stop people's tongues," he said, "and therefore the best thing to do is to stop your own ears and never mind what is spoken. There is a world of idle chitchat abroad, and he who takes note of it will have enough to do" (*Lectures to My Students*; Marshall, Morgan, and Scott reprint edition, 1965, p. 321). Of course, if we are honest, we may have to confess that we have done our share of talking about others (see Ps. 38; Matt. 7:1–3)!

Our inability to grasp the meaning of all that God is doing in this world (Eccl. 7:23–25; see 3:11; 8:17). Even Solomon with all his God-given wisdom could not understand all that exists, how God manages it, and what purposes He has in mind. He searched for the "reason [scheme] of things" but found no final answers to all his questions. However, the wise man knows that he does not know, and this is what helps to make him wise!

The sinfulness of humanity in general (Eccl. 7:26–29). Solomon began with the sinful woman, the prostitute who traps men and leads them to death (v. 26; see Prov. 2:16–19; 5:3–6; 6:24–26; 7:5–27). Solomon himself had been snared by many foreign women who enticed him away from the Lord and into the worship of heathen gods (1 Kings 11:3–8). The way to escape this evil woman is to fear God and seek to please Him.

—*Be Satisfied*, pages 107–8

7. Which of the problems listed in the previous commentary excerpt is hardest to address in our world today? How does wisdom from God help us address each one? How do we know if our wisdom is from God or from the world?

From the Commentary

> Beginning with Nimrod (Gen. 10:8–9) and continuing over the centuries through Pharaoh, Sennacherib, Nebuchadnezzar, Darius, the caesars, and the latest petty dictator, millions of good people have been oppressed in one way or another by bad rulers. The Jews often suffered at the hands of foreign oppressors, and Solomon himself was guilty of putting his own people under a heavy yoke of bondage (1 Kings 4:7–28; 12:1ff.).
>
> Keep in mind that Eastern rulers in that day held the power of life and death in their hands and often used that power capriciously. They were not elected by the people nor were they answerable to them. Some leaders ruled as benevolent dictators, but for the most part rulers in the ancient East were tyrannical despots who permitted nothing to stand in the way of fulfilling their desires.

> Solomon described an officer in the royal court, a man who had to carry out the orders of a despotic ruler. The officer had wisdom; in fact, it showed on his face (Eccl. 8:1; see Neh. 2:1ff.; Prov. 15:13). Suppose the king commanded the servant to do something evil, something that the servant did not want to do? What should the servant do? Here is where wisdom comes to his aid. His wisdom told him that there were four possible approaches he could take to this problem.
>
> —*Be Satisfied*, pages 114–15

8. Review Ecclesiastes 8:1–6. What were the possible responses the officer could have to the king's command? What is the right (wise) response? How does this sort of circumstance repeat itself in today's world? What are the ingredients that add up to good discernment?

More to Consider: Skim or read Acts 4—5. How did the apostles exercise spiritual discernment when they were arrested and persecuted?

From the Commentary

Solomon summarized his concern in Ecclesiastes 8:14: "righteous men who get what the wicked deserve, and wicked men who get what the righteous deserve" (NIV). In spite of good laws and fine people who seek to enforce them, there is more injustice in this world than we care to admit. A Spanish proverb says, "Laws, like the spider's web, catch the fly and let the hawks go free." According to famous trial lawyer F. Lee Bailey, "In America, an acquittal doesn't mean you're innocent; it means you beat the rap." His definition is a bit cynical, but poet Robert Frost defined a jury as "twelve persons chosen to decide who has the better lawyer."

In Ecclesiastes 8:10, Solomon reported on a funeral he had attended. The deceased was a man who had frequented the temple ("the place of the holy") and had received much praise from the people, but he had not lived a godly life. Yet he was given a magnificent funeral, with an eloquent eulogy, while the truly godly people of the city were ignored and forgotten.

As he reflected on the matter, Solomon realized that the deceased man had continued in his sin because he thought he was getting away with it (Eccl. 8:11). God is indeed longsuffering toward sinners and doesn't always judge sin immediately (2 Peter 3:1–12). However, God's mercy must not be used as an excuse for man's rebellion.

—*Be Satisfied*, page 118

9. Review Ecclesiastes 8:10–15. What was Solomon's answer to injustice? Why is there so much unfairness in the world today? How does our faith in God's plan help us to endure unfair situations?

From the Commentary

> The person who has to know everything, or who thinks he knows everything, is destined for disappointment in this world. Through many difficult days and sleepless nights, the Preacher applied himself diligently to the mysteries of life. He came to the conclusion that "man cannot find out the work that is done under the sun" (Eccl. 8:17; see 3:11; 7:14, 24, 27–28). Perhaps we can solve a puzzle here and there, but no man or woman can comprehend the totality of things or explain all that God is doing.
>
> Historian Will Durant surveyed human history in his multivolume *Story of Civilization* and came to the conclusion that "our knowledge is a receding mirage in an expanding desert of ignorance." Of course, this fact must not be used as an excuse for stupidity.
>
> —*Be Satisfied*, page 119

10. Read Deuteronomy 29:29. How does this verse relate to Solomon's conclusion about knowledge? What does God expect of us when it comes to knowledge? How can the pursuit of God's truth help us become wiser? (See John 7:17.)

Looking Inward

Take a moment to reflect on all that you've explored thus far in this study of Ecclesiastes 7—8. Review your notes and answers and think about how each of these things matters in your life today.

> *Tips for Small Groups: To get the most out of this section, form pairs or trios and have group members take turns answering these questions. Be honest and as open as you can in this discussion, but most of all, be encouraging and supportive of others. Be sensitive to those who are going through particularly difficult times and don't press for people to speak if they're uncomfortable doing so.*

11. When have you embraced the "praise of fools"? Why did you embrace that? What was the result? When have you encountered "wise rebukes" in life? How did you respond to those? How did those rebukes affect your life?

12. Describe a time when you were particularly discerning about a situation. Where did that discernment come from? Describe a time when you should have been discerning but weren't? What was missing?

13. Have you ever been treated unfairly? Explain. How did that circumstance affect your relationship with the people who treated you badly? How did it affect your relationship with God? What is a good and godly way to deal with the reality that life isn't fair? How can God use inequity to further His plan for you?

Going Forward

14. Think of one or two things that you have learned that you'd like to work on in the coming week. Remember that this is all about quality, not quantity. It's better to work on one specific area of life and do it well than to work on many and do poorly (or to be so overwhelmed that you simply don't try).

Do you need to become more discerning? Be specific. Go back through Ecclesiastes 7—8 and put a star next to the phrase or verse that is most encouraging to you. Consider memorizing this verse.

Real-Life Application Ideas: Discernment is a skill that is developed over time, with study and prayer and by learning to hear God's voice in circumstances. This week, talk with a spiritual mentor or church leader about how you might become more discerning in all aspects of life—as a friend, worker, spouse, parent, neighbor. Focus on those things that are currently causing you to stop, and ponder questions like "What should I do?" and "What's the right answer here?" Study God's Word, listen to wise counsel, and then take steps toward answering those questions with godly wisdom.

Seeking Help

15. Write a prayer below (or simply pray one in silence), inviting God to work on your mind and heart in those areas you've noted in the Going Forward section. Be honest about your desires and fears.

Notes for Small Groups:

- *Look for ways to put into practice the things you wrote in the Going Forward section. Talk with other group members about your ideas and commit to being accountable to one another.*
- *During the coming week, ask the Holy Spirit to continue to reveal truth to you from what you've read and studied.*
- *Before you start the next lesson, read Ecclesiastes 9—10. For more in-depth lesson preparation, read chapters 10 and 11, "Meeting Your Last Enemy" and "A Little Folly Is Dangerous," in* Be Satisfied.

Enemies

(ECCLESIASTES 9—10)

Before you begin …

- *Pray for the Holy Spirit to reveal truth and wisdom as you go through this lesson.*
- *Read Ecclesiastes 9—10. This lesson references chapters 10 and 11 in* Be Satisfied. *It will be helpful for you to have your Bible and a copy of the commentary available as you work through this lesson.*

Getting Started

From the Commentary

"I'm not afraid to die," quipped Woody Allen, "I just don't want to be there when it happens." But he *will* be there when it happens, as must every human being, because there is no escaping death when your time has come. Death is not an accident, it's an appointment (Heb. 9:27), a destiny that nobody but God can cancel or change.

Life and death are "in the hand of God" (Eccl. 9:1), and

> only He knows our future, whether it will bring blessing ("love") or sorrow ("hatred"). Solomon was not suggesting that we are passive actors in a cosmic drama, following an unchangeable script handed to us by an uncaring director. Throughout this book, Solomon has emphasized our freedom of discernment and decision. But only God knows what the future holds for us and what will happen tomorrow because of the decisions we make today.
>
> "As it is with the good man, so with the sinner" (Eccl. 9:2 NIV). "If so, why bother to live a godly life?" someone may ask. "After all, whether we obey the law or disobey, bring sacrifices or neglect them, make or break promises, we will die just the same."
>
> —*Be Satisfied*, page 124

1. Review Ecclesiastes 9:2. If this is true, why bother to live a godly life? What is Solomon's greater point here?

More to Consider: Read Romans 6:23; John 11:25–26; 1 Thessalonians 4:13–18; and 1 Corinthians 15:51–58. How do these verses give believers confidence about the future? What do these verses tell us about the nonbeliever?

2. Choose one verse or phrase from Ecclesiastes 9—10 that stands out to you. This could be something you're intrigued by, something that makes you uncomfortable, something that puzzles you, something that resonates with you, or just something you want to examine further. Write that here.

Going Deeper

From the Commentary

The fact of death and the fear of death will either bring out the best in people or the worst in people, and too often it is the worst. When death comes to a family, it doesn't *create* problems, it *reveals* them. Many ministers and funeral directors have witnessed the "X-ray" power of death and bereavement as it reveals the hearts of people. In facing the death of others, we are confronted with our own death, and many people just can't handle it.

> "The heart of the sons of men is full of evil," and that evil is bound to come out. People will do almost *anything but repent* in order to escape the reality of death. They will get drunk, fight with their relatives, drive recklessly, spend large amounts of money on useless things, and plunge into one senseless pleasure after another, all to keep the Grim Reaper at arm's length. But their costly endeavors only distract them from the battle; they don't end the war, because "the last enemy" is still there.
>
> —*Be Satisfied*, page 125

3. Why does death (of a family member, friend, coworker, etc.) reveal truth about the living? How did Solomon address this? Why are we as a culture so obsessed with death? What does this say about the role of faith in our nation?

From the Commentary

> When confronted by the stern fact of death, not everybody dives into an escape hatch and shouts, "Let's eat, drink, and be merry, for tomorrow we die!" Many people

just grit their teeth, square their shoulders, and endure. They hold on to that ancient motto, "Where there's life, there's hope!" (That's a good paraphrase of Eccl. 9:4.)

That motto goes as far back as the third century BC. It's part of a conversation between two farmers who are featured in a poem by the Greek poet Theokritos. "Console yourself, dear Battos," says Korydon. "Things may be better tomorrow. While there's life, there's hope. Only the dead have none." Shades of Ecclesiastes!

Solomon would be the last person to discourage anybody from hoping for the best. Better to be a living dog (and dogs were despised in that day) than a dead lion.

—*Be Satisfied*, page 126

4. Who is the primary audience for Solomon's "where there's life, there's hope" message? What did Solomon say about tempering that hope?

From the Commentary

> Enjoyment has been one of Solomon's recurring themes (Eccl. 2:24; 3:12–15, 22; 5:18–20; 8:15), and he will bring it up again (11:9–10). His admonition "Go thy way!" means: "Don't sit around and brood! Get up and live!" Yes, death is coming, but God gives us good gifts to enjoy, so enjoy them!
>
> Solomon didn't urge us to join the "jet set" and start searching for exotic pleasures in faraway places. Instead, he listed some of the common experiences of home life: happy, leisurely meals (Eccl. 9:7); joyful family celebrations (v. 8); a faithful, loving marriage (v. 9); and hard work (v. 10).
>
> —*Be Satisfied*, page 127

5. Why did Solomon focus on the common experiences of life in Ecclesiastes 9:7–10? How does this compare with modern society's formula for happiness? What might Solomon say about our modern schedules and priorities?

From the Commentary

> Anticipating the response of his listeners (and his readers), Solomon turned from his discussion of death and began to discuss life. "If death is unavoidable," somebody would argue, "then the smartest thing we can do is major on our strengths and concentrate on life. When death comes, at least we'll have the satisfaction of knowing we worked hard and achieved some success."
>
> "Don't be too sure of that!" was Solomon's reply. "You can't guarantee what will happen in life, because life is unpredictable."
>
> While it is generally true that the fastest runners win the races, the strongest soldiers win the battles, and the smartest and most skillful workers win the best jobs, it is also true that these same gifted people can fail miserably because of factors out of their control. The successful person knows how to make the most of "time and procedure" (Eccl. 8:5 NIV), but only the Lord can control "time and chance" (9:11).
>
> —*Be Satisfied*, page 130

6. Review Ecclesiastes 9:11–18. What message is there in this passage for today's go-getters? Why did Solomon issue this caution? Doesn't this serve to demotivate people? Why or why not? What does this caution reveal about God's role in our daily lives?

From the Commentary

> It is not clear whether the wise man in Ecclesiastes 9:13–18 actually delivered the city, or whether he could have saved it and was asked but did not heed. I lean toward the second explanation because it fits in better with verses 16–18. (The Hebrew allows for the translation "could have"; see the verse 15 footnote in the NASB.) The little city was besieged and the wise man could have delivered it, but nobody paid any attention to him. Verse 17 suggests that a ruler with a loud mouth got all of the attention and led the people into defeat. The wise man spoke quietly and was ignored. He had the opportunity for greatness but was frustrated by one loud, ignorant man.
>
> —*Be Satisfied*, page 131

7. Read one or more of these passages: Genesis 3; Romans 5; Joshua 7; 2 Samuel 15—18; 2 Samuel 24. How do these passages support the truth of Solomon's conclusion in Ecclesiastes 9:18? Why does wisdom often speak quietly while foolishness has a loud voice?

From the Commentary

> Before he concluded his message, Solomon thought it wise to remind his congregation once again of the importance of wisdom and the danger of folly. (The word for "folly" is used nine times in Ecclesiastes 10.) In verse 1, he laid down the basic principle that folly creates problems for those who commit it. He had already compared a good name to fragrant perfume (7:1), so he used the image again. What dead flies are to perfume, folly is to the reputation of the wise person. The conclusion is logical: Wise people will stay away from folly!
>
> —*Be Satisfied*, page 135

8. According to Solomon, what makes one person foolish and another wise? (See Eccl. 10:2; Prov. 4:23.) What are the greatest dangers of folly? How can we discern the difference between wisdom and foolishness?

More to Consider: In the ancient world, the right hand was the place of power and honor, while the left hand represented weakness and rejection (Matt. 25:33, 41). Solomon referenced this in Ecclesiastes 10:2. What does the inclusion of these sorts of cultural references tell us about how we ought to interpret Scripture? What are some examples of modern idioms relating to our faith life that future generations might struggle with unless they understood our culture?

From the Commentary

If there is one person who needs wisdom, it is the ruler of a nation. When God asked Solomon what gift he especially wanted, the king asked for wisdom (1 Kings 3:3–28). Lyndon B. Johnson said, "A president's hardest task is not to *do* what's right, but to *know* what's right." That requires wisdom.

If a ruler is *proud*, he may say and do foolish things that cause him to lose the respect of his associates. The picture here is of a proud ruler who easily becomes angry and takes out his anger on the attendants around him. Of course, if a man has no control over himself, how can he hope to have control over his people? "He who is slow to anger is better than the mighty, and he who rules his spirit than he who takes a city" (Prov. 16:32 NKJV). "Whoever has no rule over his own spirit is like a city broken down, without walls" (Prov. 25:28 NKJV).

However, it isn't necessary for his servants to act like fools! In fact, that's the worst thing they can do (Eccl. 8:3). Far better that they control themselves, stay right where they are, and seek to bring peace.

To be sure, there is a righteous anger that sometimes needs to be displayed (Eph. 4:26), but not everything we call "righteous indignation" is really "righteous."

—*Be Satisfied*, page 136

9. Read Proverbs 16:14 and 25:15. How do these passages speak to the issue Solomon raised concerning a proud leader? How do we experience similar challenges in today's world? What is the difference between righteous anger and unrighteous anger?

From the Commentary

In the book of Proverbs, Solomon had much to say about the speech of fools. In Ecclesiastes 10:12–15, he pointed out four characteristics of their words.

(1) Destructive (v. 12). The wise person will speak gracious words that are suited to the listeners and the occasion (Prov. 10:32; 25:11). Whether in personal conversation or public ministry, our Lord always knew the right thing to say at the right time (Isa. 50:4). We should try to emulate Him. But the fool blurts out whatever is on his mind and doesn't stop to consider who might be hurt by it. In the end, it is the fool himself who is hurt the most: "a fool is consumed by his own lips" (Eccl. 10:12 NIV).

(2) Unreasonable (v. 13). What he says doesn't make sense. And the longer he talks, the crazier it becomes. "The beginning of his talking is folly and the end of it is wicked madness" (NASB). He would be better off to keep quiet, because all that he says only lets everybody know that he is a fool (5:3). Paul called these people "unruly and vain talkers" (Titus 1:10), which J. B. Phillips translates "who will not recognize authority, who talk nonsense" (PH).

(3) Uncontrolled (v. 14a). The fool is "full of words" without realizing that he is saying nothing. "In the multitude of words sin is not lacking, but he who restrains his lips is wise" (Prov. 10:19 NKJV). The person who can control his or her tongue is able to discipline the entire body (James 3:1–2). Jesus said, "But let your 'Yes' be 'Yes' and your 'No,' 'No.' For whatever is more than this is from the evil one" (Matt. 5:37 NKJV).

(4) Boastful (14b–15). Foolish people talk about the future as though they either know all about it or are in control of what will happen. "Do not boast about tomorrow, for you do not know what a day may bring forth" (Prov. 27:1 NKJV). Several times before, Solomon has emphasized man's ignorance of the future (Eccl. 3:22; 6:12; 8:7; 9:12), a truth that wise people receive but fools reject (see James 4:13–17).

—*Be Satisfied*, pages 139–40

10. How do Solomon's four characteristics of a fool's speech apply to our world today? What cautions does this give us for the church? What happens when people in positions of authority exhibit these characteristics? What is the proper and biblical way to confront leaders who are foolish with their speech?

Looking Inward

Take a moment to reflect on all that you've explored thus far in this study of Ecclesiastes 9—10. Review your notes and answers and think about how each of these things matters in your life today.

Tips for Small Groups: To get the most out of this section, form pairs or trios and have group members take turns answering these questions. Be honest and as open as you can in this discussion, but most of all, be encouraging and supportive of others. Be sensitive to those who are going through particularly difficult times and don't press for people to speak if they're uncomfortable doing so.

11. How often do you think about death? What does the way you respond to the death of a loved one or friend reveal about you? How is your faith in God affected by the death of someone you love?

12. Solomon stated that where there's life, there's hope. What are some of the ways you're holding on to hope today? How does your faith inform your hope? How do you keep a balance between being hopeful and being realistic?

13. When have you had to deal with a foolish leader or foolish speech? How did you respond? What are the greatest challenges of working for someone with whom you disagree? How do you know when it's time to speak out about a leader's foolishness and when it's time to be quiet?

Going Forward

14. Think of one or two things that you have learned that you'd like to work on in the coming week. Remember that this is all about quality, not quantity. It's better to work on one specific area of life and do it well than to work on many and do poorly (or to be so overwhelmed that you simply don't try).

Do you want to do a better job of holding on to hope when life gets hard? Be specific. Go back through Ecclesiastes 9—10 and put a star next to the phrase or verse that is most encouraging to you. Consider memorizing this verse.

Real-Life Application Ideas: Solomon talks a lot about the importance of enjoying life because it's fleeting. This week, come up with two or three ways to truly embrace the gift of life God has given you. This might be as simple as going for a walk in a park or taking that leap of faith and trying out for the worship team. Be bold and pursue the enjoyment of life in God-honoring ways. Then take time to thank God for every minute you've been granted.

Seeking Help

15. Write a prayer below (or simply pray one in silence), inviting God to work on your mind and heart in those areas you've noted in the Going Forward section. Be honest about your desires and fears.

Notes for Small Groups:

- *Look for ways to put into practice the things you wrote in the Going Forward section. Talk with other group members about your ideas and commit to being accountable to one another.*
- *During the coming week, ask the Holy Spirit to continue to reveal truth to you from what you've read and studied.*
- *Before you start the next lesson, read Ecclesiastes 11—12. For more in-depth lesson preparation, read chapter 12, "What Life Is All About," in* Be Satisfied.

What It's All About

(ECCLESIASTES 11—12)

Before you begin …

- *Pray for the Holy Spirit to reveal truth and wisdom as you go through this lesson.*
- *Read Ecclesiastes 11—12. This lesson references chapter 12 in* Be Satisfied. *It will be helpful for you to have your Bible and a copy of the commentary available as you work through this lesson.*

Getting Started

From the Commentary

"Is life worth living?"

That was the question the Preacher raised when he began the discourse that we call Ecclesiastes. After experimenting and investigating "life under the sun," he concluded, "No, life is *not* worth living!" He gave four arguments to support his conclusion: the monotony of life, the vanity of wisdom, the futility of wealth, and the certainty of death.

> Being a wise man, Solomon reviewed his arguments and this time brought God into the picture. What a difference it made. He realized that life was not monotonous but filled with challenging situations from God, each in its own time and each for its own purpose. He also learned that wealth could be enjoyed and employed to the glory of God.
>
> —*Be Satisfied*, page 147

1. What were Solomon's conclusions after all his exploration of folly and wisdom? Of the meaning of life? What can we take away from Ecclesiastes in regard to how we live our daily lives?

2. Choose one verse or phrase from Ecclesiastes 11—12 that stands out to you. This could be something you're intrigued by, something that makes you uncomfortable, something that puzzles you, something that resonates with you, or just something you want to examine further. Write that here.

Going Deeper

From the Commentary

Solomon was ready for his conclusion and personal application. What he did was present *four pictures of life* and attach to each picture a practical admonition for his listeners (and readers) to heed. The development looks like this:

Life is an *adventure*—live by faith (Eccl. 11:1–6).

Life is a *gift*—enjoy it (Eccl. 11:7—12:8).

Life is a *school*—learn your lessons (Eccl. 12:9–12).

Life is a *stewardship*—fear God (Eccl. 12:13–14).

These four pictures parallel the four arguments that Solomon wrestled with throughout the book. Life is not monotonous; rather, it is an adventure of faith that is anything but predictable or tedious. Yes, death is certain, but life is a gift from God and He wants us to enjoy it. Are there questions we can't answer and problems we can't solve? Don't despair. God teaches us His truth as we advance in "the school of life," and He will give us wisdom enough to make sensible decisions. Finally, as far as wealth is concerned, all of life is a stewardship from God, and one day He will call us to give an account. Therefore, "fear God, and keep his commandments" (Eccl. 12:13).

—*Be Satisfied*, pages 147–48

3. Review the four pictures of life listed in the previous commentary excerpt. Why is each of these pictures important? Which of these seems hardest for today's believers to embrace? Explain.

From the Commentary

When I was a boy, I practically lived in the public library during the summer months. I loved books, the building was cool, and the librarians gave me the run of the place since I was one of their best customers. One summer I read nothing but true adventure stories written by real heroes like Frank Buck and Martin Johnson. These men knew the African jungles better than I knew my hometown! I was fascinated by *I Married Adventure*, the autobiography of Martin Johnson's wife, Osa. When Clyde Beatty brought his circus to town, I was in the front row watching him "tame" the lions.

Since those boyhood days, life has become a lot calmer for me, but I trust I haven't lost that sense of adventure.

In fact, as I get older, I'm asking God to keep me from getting set in my ways in a life that is routine, boring, and predictable. "I don't want my life to end in a swamp," said British expositor F. B. Meyer. I agree with him. When I trusted Jesus Christ as my Savior, "I married adventure," and that meant living by faith and expecting the unexpected.

—*Be Satisfied*, pages 148–49

4. Solomon used two activities to illustrate his point about life being an adventure: a merchant sending out ships (Eccl. 11:1–2) and a farmer sowing seed (vv. 3–6). What do these illustrations reveal about life as adventure? What do they reveal about the role of faith in that life adventure?

More to Consider: If you are looking for an excuse to do nothing, you can find one. Athlete and evangelist Billy Sunday said an excuse is "the skin of a reason stuffed with a lie." Life is an adventure, and often we must launch out by faith, even when the circumstances seem adverse. Read John 3:8; Psalm 139:14–15; and Ecclesiastes 3:1–11. What do these verses tell us about living by faith?

From Today's World

In addition to being an entertainment-soaked culture, we're also a culture obsessed with adventure. Some of the most popular movies and books and TV series are action-packed adventures. People pay lots of money to enjoy real adventures (safaris, hang gliding, bungee jumping) and pretend ones (theme parks, video games). Adventure brings with it the promise of thrills and unforgettable experiences.

5. What is the best thing about this adventure-focused world we live in? What challenges does it present? How can we view our faith life as an adventure? How might that kind of thinking change the way we live out our faith?

From the Commentary

> Solomon's sixth and final admonition is that we accept life as a gift and learn to enjoy all that God shares with us (see Eccl. 2:24; 3:12–15, 22; 5:18–20; 8:15; 9:7–10). In order to do this, we must obey three instructions: rejoice (11:7–9), remove (11:10), and remember (12:1–8).
>
> The first instruction, rejoice, is described in Ecclesiastes 11:7–9. What a joy it is to anticipate each new day and

> accept it as a fresh gift from God! I confess that I never realized what it meant to live a day at a time until I was nearly killed in an auto accident back in 1966. It was caused by a drunk driver careening around a curve between eighty and ninety miles per hour. By the grace of God, I had no serious injuries; but my stay in the intensive care ward, and my time of recuperation at home, made me a firm believer in Deuteronomy 33:25: "As thy days, so shall thy strength be." Now when I awaken early each morning, I thank God for the new day, and I ask Him to help me use it wisely for His glory and to enjoy it as His gift.
>
> —*Be Satisfied*, page 151

6. What does "rejoicing" look like in everyday life? What are some ways believers can enjoy the "days of youth" Solomon referred to? Was Solomon saying there is no joy later in life? Explain.

From the Commentary

> The second instruction, remove, is described in Ecclesiastes 11:10. Privileges must be balanced by personal

responsibilities. Young people must put anxiety out of their hearts (Matt. 6:24–34) and evil away from their flesh (2 Cor. 7:1). The word translated "sorrow" means "vexation, inner pain, anxiety." If we are living in the will of God, we will have the peace of God in our hearts (Phil. 4:6–9). The sins of the flesh only destroy the body and can bring eternal judgment to the soul.

The phrase "childhood and youth are vanity" does not mean that these stages in life are unimportant and a waste of time. Quite the opposite is true! The best way to have a happy adult life and a contented old age is to get a good start early in life and avoid the things that will bring trouble later on. Young people who take care of their minds and bodies, avoid the destructive sins of the flesh, and build good habits of health and holiness have a better chance for happy adult years than those who "sow their wild oats" and pray for a crop failure.

The third instruction, remember (Eccl. 12:1–8), means more than "think about God." It means "pay attention to, consider with the intention of obeying." It is Solomon's version of Matthew 6:33: "But seek first the kingdom of God and His righteousness" (NKJV). How easy it is to neglect the Lord when you are caught up in the enjoyments and opportunities of youth. We know that dark days (Eccl. 11:8) and difficult [evil] days (12:1) are coming, so we had better lay a good spiritual foundation as early in life as possible. During our youthful years, the sky is bright (11:7), but the time will come when there will be darkness and one storm after another.

—*Be Satisfied*, pages 152–53

7. How are the second and third instructions (remove and remember) related to the first one, rejoice? What does the phrase "childhood and youth are vanity" (vapor, mist) mean in this context? Why is it important to "remember" as we live our lives? How do all three of these instructions—rejoice, remove, and remember—help us live fulfilling lives?

From the Commentary

Someone has said that life is like a school, except that sometimes you don't know what the lessons are until you have failed the examination. God teaches us primarily from His Word; but He also teaches us through creation, history, and the various experiences of life. Solomon explained the characteristics of his own work as a teacher of God's truth.

Solomon was the wisest of men (1 Kings 3:3–28). The king studied and explored many subjects, and some of his conclusions he wrote down in Proverbs.

> After studying a matter, he weighed his conclusions carefully, and then arranged them in an orderly fashion. His whole approach was certainly scientific. We may not always see the pattern behind his arrangement, but it is there just the same.
>
> Solomon sought to be *careful* in his teaching, so he used "acceptable words." This means "pleasing" or "gracious" words (Eccl. 10:12) that would win the attention of his listeners and readers. However, at no time did he dilute his message or flatter his congregation. He always used *upright words of truth* (see Prov. 8:6–11). Like our Lord Jesus Christ, the king was able to combine "grace and truth" (John 1:17; Luke 4:16–32).
>
> The Preacher claimed that his words were *inspired*, given by God, the One Shepherd. Inspiration was the special miracle ministry of the Holy Spirit that enabled men of God to write the Word of God as God wanted it written, complete and without error (2 Tim. 3:16–17; 2 Peter 1:20–21).
>
> —*Be Satisfied*, page 155

8. Why is it important that Solomon was careful in his teaching? What does it look like to be a careful teacher today? For us to trust Solomon's words, we must believe they're inspired by God. How do we know when someone is speaking inspired words today?

More to Consider: If life is a school, then the Holy Spirit is our teacher. Read John 14:26; 15:26; 16:12–15; Psalm 119:97–104; and 2 Peter 3:18. What does each of these passages tell us about our teacher and what we ought to be learning?

From the Commentary

> Ecclesiastes ends where the book of Proverbs begins (Prov. 1:7), with an admonition for us to fear the Lord (see Eccl. 3:14; 5:7; 7:18; 8:12–13). The "fear of the Lord" is that attitude of reverence and awe that His people show to Him because they love Him and respect His power and His greatness. The person who fears the Lord will pay attention to His Word and obey it. He or she will not tempt the Lord by deliberately disobeying or by "playing with sin." An unholy fear makes people run away from God, but a holy fear brings them to their knees in loving submission to God.
>
> —*Be Satisfied*, pages 156–57

9. Review Ecclesiastes 12:13. What does it mean to be the stewards of our lives and not the owners? How does that change our perspectives on daily living? What does fearing the Lord look like in daily living?

From the Commentary

> "The eternity of punishment is a thought which crushes the heart," said Charles Spurgeon. "The Lord God is slow to anger, but when he is once aroused to it, as he will be against those who finally reject his Son, he will put forth all his omnipotence to crush his enemies."
>
> Six times in his discourse, Solomon told us to enjoy life while we can; but at no time did he advise us to enjoy sin. If you know Jesus Christ as your Savior, then your sins have already been judged on the cross, and "there is therefore now no condemnation to them which are in Christ Jesus" (Rom. 8:1; and see John 5:24). But if you die having never trusted Christ, you will face judgment at His throne and be lost forever (Rev. 20:11–15).
>
> —*Be Satisfied*, page 158

10. Respond to the following statement: The joys of the present depend on the security of the future. How does this align with Solomon's overarching message about the meaning of life?

Looking Inward

Take a moment to reflect on all that you've explored thus far in this study of Ecclesiastes 11—12. Review your notes and answers and think about how each of these things matters in your life today.

Tips for Small Groups: To get the most out of this section, form pairs or trios and have group members take turns answering these questions. Be honest and as open as you can in this discussion, but most of all, be encouraging and supportive of others. Be sensitive to those who are going through particularly difficult times and don't press for people to speak if they're uncomfortable doing so.

11. What are some ways you embrace life as an adventure? How does doing this glorify God? If you're not enjoying the adventure, what can you do to change that?

12. What does it mean to you to be a steward of your life and not an owner of it? Do you live this way? Why or why not? Where does your faith fit into this puzzle?

13. What does "fearing the Lord" mean to you? How is that different from being afraid of God? What does it look like to fear the Lord in everyday life? How does this acknowledgment that God is in control impact your decision making?

Going Forward

14. Think of one or two things that you have learned that you'd like to work on in the coming week. Remember that this is all about quality, not quantity. It's better to work on one specific area of life and do it well than to work on many and do poorly (or to be so overwhelmed that you simply don't try).

Do you want to learn how to embrace life as a gift from God? Be specific. Go back through Ecclesiastes 11—12 and put a star next to the phrase or verse that is most encouraging to you. Consider memorizing this verse.

Real-Life Application Ideas: Solomon's examination of life ultimately leads us to see that life without God is meaningless and that life with God is a grand adventure that is satisfying and ultimately wonderful, no matter what we go through from birth to death. This is a great reminder for believers to embrace the gift of life God has given them. But it's also a stark reminder of what those who don't believe are missing. Use this message as a prompter to be more intentional this week in sharing your faith. Look for opportunities to tell nonbelievers that you've earned the right to talk about the great adventure that awaits them, too. Then trust God to do the rest.

Seeking Help

15. Write a prayer below (or simply pray one in silence), inviting God to work on your mind and heart in those areas you've noted in the Going Forward section. Be honest about your desires and fears.

Notes for Small Groups:

- *Look for ways to put into practice the things you wrote in the Going Forward section. Talk with other group members about your ideas and commit to being accountable to one another.*
- *During the coming week, ask the Holy Spirit to continue to reveal truth to you from what you've read and studied.*

Summary and Review

Notes for Small Groups: This session is a summary and review of this book. Because of that, it is shorter than the previous lessons. If you are using this in a small-group setting, consider combining this lesson with a time of fellowship or a shared meal.

Before you begin ...

- *Pray for the Holy Spirit to reveal truth and wisdom as you go through this lesson.*
- *Briefly review the notes you made in the previous sessions. You will refer back to previous sections throughout this bonus lesson.*

Looking Back

1. Over the past eight lessons, you've examined the book of Ecclesiastes. What expectations did you bring to this study? In what ways were those expectations met?

2. What is the most significant personal discovery you've made from this study?

3. What surprised you most about Ecclesiastes? What, if anything, troubled you?

Progress Report

4. Take a few moments to review the Going Forward sections of the previous lessons. How would you rate your progress for each of the things you chose to work on? What adjustments, if any, do you need to make to continue on the path toward spiritual maturity?

5. In what ways have you grown closer to Christ during this study? Take a moment to celebrate those things. Then think of areas where you feel you still need to grow and note those here. Make plans to revisit this study in a few weeks to review your growing faith.

Things to Pray About

6. Ecclesiastes is a book about the meaning of life. As you reflect on this theme, consider what it means to be truly satisfied in this life.

7. The messages in Ecclesiastes are all huge—life, death, wisdom, foolishness. Spend time praying to better understand what God put on Solomon's heart in this very important book of the Bible.

8. Whether you've been studying this in a small group or on your own, there are many other Christians working through the very same issues you discovered when examining Ecclesiastes. Take time to pray for them, that God would reveal truth, that the Holy Spirit would guide you, and that each person might grow in spiritual maturity according to God's will.

A Blessing of Encouragement

Studying the Bible is one of the best ways to learn how to be more like Christ. Thanks for taking this step. In closing, let this blessing precede you and follow you into the next week while you continue to marinate in God's Word:

May God light your path to greater understanding as you review the truths found in Ecclesiastes and consider how they can help you grow closer to Christ.